Dream

CW00693221

This

Is Why

I'm Here

A Practical Guide to Discovering Your
Purpose and Nurturing Your Dreams

MICHAEL V. IVANOV

Dream Big! _Mike_ (handwritten inscription)

ISBN-13: 979-8-9853041-6-9

For speaking inquiries, please visit Michael's website below

Special discounts are available on quantity purchases by corporations, associations, and others. For details, contact the publisher at the web address below.

www.SPEAKLIFE365.com

Dedicated to all those who persevere in pursuing their dreams.
Never ever give up!

Sincerely,
Michael

Other books by Michael V. Ivanov

The Mount of Olives:
11 Declarations to an Extraordinary Life

The Traveler's Secret:
Ancient Proverbs for Better Living

The Servant With One Talent:
Five Success Principles from the Greatest Parable
Ever Told

The Cabin at the End of the Train:
A Story About Pursuing Dreams

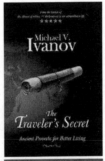

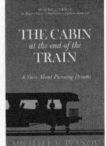

Contents

One   Why am I here?   1

Two   Limiting Beliefs   13

Three   Big Idea #1: BELIEVE IN YOURSELF   26

Four   Big Idea #2: BELIEVE IN OTHERS   58

Five   Big Idea #3: THINK BIG   83

Six   Big Idea #4: NEVER EVER GIVE UP   104

About the Author   128

Discover more books from Michael   130

One

Why am I here?

It was a hot June day just before the end of fifth grade, and I was walking home from school. Just a few blocks from my house, a huge kid named Kyle and his equally giant step-brother, Anthony, caught up to me. For months, Kyle had been calling me a "Commie," a "Russian spy," and screaming, "Go back to your own country!" every time he passed me in the hallways. Once, he even kicked the lunch tray out of my hands and pretended it was an accident. That was all he could do to me at school since adults were always nearby. Now, we were off school property.

It was me against two of the biggest fifth graders our little town had ever produced. I was positive they had both been born near a nuclear plant—these two ugly giants already had armpit hair.

Anthony gripped me by my backpack and pounded the back of my head while Kyle turned his fists into a windmill and aimed for my face. I ducked my head, punched, and kicked at his gut with everything I had.

They were fully prepared to beat me to a pulp, but I managed to put up a fight until an old lady mowing her lawn yelled at us to break up the fight.

When I got home, I went straight to my room and cried. I kicked and punched my mattress until I was exhausted, wishing it was Kyle's fat face. There was no way I would tell my mom about what happened because she would tell Dad, and Dad would call the school the next day. Then, I would get more beatings from the two over-sized terrorists.

I didn't cry because I was in pain. I cried out of frustration. I didn't know why it mattered that I was born in another country or that I spoke a different language. Until they started bullying me, I never had the slightest idea there was ever anything "wrong" with me. I didn't know anything about the Cold War. And I certainly didn't know what a "Commie" was.

In fact, I *loved* sharing that I was born in Ukraine and moved to America just before the collapse of the Soviet Union. Anytime we did presentations at school about ourselves or our family, I told how my grandfather fought for the Red Army in World War II and survived four years in the Nazi's Dachau Concentration camp. I always thought that was pretty cool. Because of my grandfather, I grew up believing our family was invincible. He was my hero, and I was proud of my family story.

But after that day, and many more like it, I realized that I didn't need to do anything wrong to have haters. As proud as I was of my family history, being an immigrant just rubbed some people the wrong way. I began to hide that part of me and stopped being proud of it.

I quickly learned that blending in with the herd was how I would survive middle school, high school, and my neighborhood: less individuality and more pretending to be like everybody else.

That's how easily the world can change who you are. It does not take much to feel unseen and unaccepted. All it takes is a few ignorant bullies, and you learn it's best to blend in instead of stand out.

I became a chameleon. I paid close attention to what everyone else was interested in and pretended to be interested in that thing, too. I carried around a skateboard because that's what the cool kids did. I cussed at school because the cool kids cussed. I stole from Walmart because kids at school were stealing from Walmart, too.

And I would have become a drug dealer, too, if I hadn't been broke. The kids who sold weed at school told me I could triple my money if I bought in for 300 bucks and helped with the distribution. But really, I didn't care about the cash; I only wanted to be seen and accepted into the herd. I wanted the bad boy attitude and behavior that gained them so much respect.

These are only a few examples among thousands like it in

my life that led me to develop the *limiting belief* that I would never be seen and accepted unless I imitated or impressed others. I believed that I needed to find a way to stand out, but not too much—I had to follow the rules of the crowd.

Can you relate? Your experiences might look different, but the results are always the same. From our grade school bullies to our office coworkers, society teaches us very quickly that the acceptance of the herd is of utmost importance. Sometimes, we'll put aside personal values, convictions, and even dreams to be accepted by the herd, even if it's the wrong herd. Think about it. If you're honest with yourself, there are probably hundreds of times you've hesitated to speak up or stand up out of fear of what everyone in the room might think.

Guess what happens when you try too hard to be like everybody else? You lose sight of who you are and what is most important to you. You downplay your uniqueness and disqualify your talents, abilities, and personality; eventually, when you no longer feel like the unique individual miracle you are, you lose your purpose. Imagine that. What an awful way to live!

Inside you and me is an unquenchable desire to do something great with our lives, pave our way, and leave our mark on the world. It's as if, at birth, we know we were destined for more. But the fear of stepping out and risking everything to explore that desire is too much. The herds we often cling to would rather we stay small, manageable, and predictable. Our ambitions remind people of their stagnation. So we play small instead, not to ruffle too many feathers.

Don't get me wrong; we need to be a part of a community. In later chapters, I discuss the necessity of a strong, supportive community around you if you want to realize your greatest potential. Herds provide safety. Community is good. And you have to live by the community's rules to stay a part of it.

For example, if today, I suggest to all of my friends that we should eat at my favorite restaurant and they all agree, even if not all of them like it as much as I do, I will be happy. But then, if one of my friends suggests we all eat at his favorite place tomorrow and I don't come because I don't like that place, I have just broken an essential rule of the herd. To be in and stay a part of a community requires some healthy compromise for the sake of others. I can't always have it my way. If I only participate in the herd's activities as long as they benefit me, I will be outside looking in very soon.

If there is a big project at school or the office, and I cherry-pick the assignments or take the easiest job and leave the most challenging jobs to my coworkers or classmates, I will quickly find myself with many haters. The unspoken rules of the herd say it's crucial to carry your weight and be accommodating and protective of others in the herd.

Be careful, however, to never let your desire to be accepted force you to compromise on your values, beliefs, convictions, and dreams. Suppose your friends are causing you to abandon your values, making you feel like you have to fight for acceptance, or the people in your office are rejecting you simply because of who you are, where you're from, or what you stand for. In that case, it's time to find another "herd."

You can't ever let the world chip away at who you are; don't exchange your dreams for the safety of a herd. Don't diminish yourself to make others feel comfortable in their mediocrity.

I'm glad you picked up this book. Maybe you've also been beaten down to the point where you feel like an ordinary face in a sea of a billion ordinary people and know that just isn't true. Or maybe you believe there is nothing special enough about you for the world to notice, and you hope that I can convince you otherwise. Perhaps you're just tired of wearing all the different masks you must put on any time you step out of the house, and you're hoping that something I might say will permit you to be yourself. Or maybe you have a sense of your greatness, but the bullies, opinions of others, and the herd standards have built a cage of fear around you, and you're terrified to open the latch. Maybe now you're ready to step out and try once more.

This is why I'm here, my friend.

Why am I here? Even during my adolescence, while I was busy masterfully blending into every environment, trying to be who people wanted me to be, attempting to run with the herd, deep down, I craved a deeper meaning. Sometimes, a preacher would speak about purpose, or my dad would tell stories from the old days, and a little voice would rise in me: *So what about me? What impact will I have on this world? What is my purpose? How will I be remembered? Why am I here?*

Something was constantly calling me to keep searching for the answers. Something was always drawing me away from small-minded people and towards something extraordinary. And no matter how far I strayed from my values to belong, the little voice never disappeared.

I often wished someone could tell me my purpose in those days. Maybe then I could stop trying to fit in where I didn't belong and please people I didn't like. I just wanted to know what I was supposed to do in life and who I was supposed to be. I knew there was an answer. At least everyone told me there was one. I thought I'd be an old man when I finally figured it out, and my purpose would be useless by then.

How come the answer to life's biggest question doesn't

come when we seem to need it most? How come birth certificates aren't accompanied by a purpose certificate? *Name, date of birth, place of birth, and reason for existence.* Wouldn't that be nice? Don't you think there would be many more happy people if each of us knew why we were here and what we should do with our lives? I suspect there would be. I agree with what Mark Twain wrote: *"The two most important days in your life are the day you were born and the day you find out why."*

That is precisely why I am beyond excited to share my journey with you, my friend. To my pleasant surprise, the answer came to me one day, and my life was never the same again. I want the same for you.

***

By the end of this book, I want you to have the mental fortitude, resolve, and resilience to keep fighting for your dreams, no matter your current environment or circumstances. No matter where you've been or what you have gone through. No matter how many times you've failed or been knocked down. Whether you're still navigating high school or coming up on your forty-year reunion, I want to equip you to do extraordinary things through your newfound purpose.

Having *mental fortitude* means you will become a master

over your fears, doubts, and negative emotions through positive thinking. Having *resolve* means you will be fully committed to taking action and achieving your dreams. Having *resilience* means you can adapt and overcome anything or anyone who tries to distract or keep you down.

And, mostly, I want to help you find an answer to that critical question, "Why am I here?" Trust me, it is never too soon or too late to start searching for your answers.

Because the truth is, I can't be there when an injury derails your life plans. I can't be there when you lose someone you love. I can't be there on those lonely nights when you wonder if anyone would even care if you were gone. I can't be there for you when your heart is broken. I can't protect you from the words of parents, teachers, preachers, bosses, spouses, or peers who intentionally or unintentionally squash your dreams. I can't be there to ease the pressure and anxiety of finding your place in this world, whether it's for the first time or whether you are starting over. And I can't pluck those negative thoughts out of your head when they creep in.

What I can do is share a few things that will help you navigate these critical years of your life. And just like a warrior preparing for battle dons a helmet, straps body armor over his chest, picks up a shield to defend himself, and takes up a sword to fight for what he believes in, you will be equipped with these tools for when you need them most.

Your life is a precious gift. You are unique. You are talented, funny, weird, shy one day and outgoing the next, artistic, and kind. There is greatness and brilliance in you. And the more of your true self you bring to the world, the better a place it will be for all of us.

That's why I can't afford to let you live this life without finding a way to bring the best out of you.

When you don't learn to protect yourself from the negativity the world will throw at you, life will seem less like a gift and more like a battle. Too many people try to take on life ill-prepared and ill-equipped, and they suffer for it. Instead of bending and shaping the world into something much more beautiful around them, they let the world bend, break, and eventually shape them.

They become so beaten down by life that they stop getting back up. I know you know people like this. They forget how much of a gift they are. They don't believe in what's possible anymore. They become full of blame, complaints, and resentment. Their obstacles become their excuses, and they turn their backs on all of their dreams. They settle for the ordinary. And that oh-so-important question, "Why am I here?" goes unanswered.

This will not be you, my friend. Not if I have something to say about it.

***

In this book, I'll share four big ideas to equip you for success. These ideas are not mind-blowing or new, nor are they a bunch of inspirational one-liners and old principles wrapped in new packaging. These are things I've learned along the way that I wish someone had shared with me when I was trying to figure out my place in this world.

If you take these ideas as your own, you'll maintain a positive mindset through the ups and downs of life. You'll have the courage to face and conquer your biggest fears. You'll be empowered to do things you never believed you could do. And you will overcome failure and rejection no matter how often you've failed because those past attempts, losses, and mistakes DO NOT define you. You will stay aware of what's most beautiful and important in life and know the brilliant gifts, skills, talents, and abilities you possess. These ideas will pave the path to an extraordinary life.

When I began to look at my life through the lens of these four big ideas, I was able to believe in myself again and achieve many of my biggest dreams. I still have much more I want to accomplish, and I know the four big ideas are guiding me along my journey. For quite some time, my biggest dream has been to become an author and a motivational speaker. And today, I get to speak in schools and conferences all over the country. I talk to students, adults, athletes, business professionals, and people from all walks of life, young and old, and I get to inspire readers worldwide through my books. Currently, my books are being translated into several different languages. How cool is that?

Through my work, I get to remind people all over the world that their life is a gift and there is a purpose for it, and I help them unbury their buried talents. It's not just why I'm here—it's also the best job I ever had.

I am living proof that you can turn your insecurities into confidence, doubts into certainties, anxiety into peace, fears into victories, and failures into success. If you believe, really believe, and take to heart the ideas I will share with you, any self-hate that festers within you will melt into self-love. Any self-doubt you carry will forge into self-confidence. Any self-sabotage you've inflicted upon yourself will morph into a hunger for self-improvement.

It did for me.

So, if you are ready, raise your hand right now, and even though you might feel silly, say out loud, "I'm ready!"

Two

Limiting Beliefs

As he walked past an enclosure housing several massive elephants, the man couldn't help but notice a peculiar sight. These powerful and enormous creatures were only tethered by a small rope around one of their front legs. There were no imposing chains or cages—just this fragile-looking restraint. His curiosity piqued; he wondered why these massive animals, capable of great strength, didn't attempt to break free.

He approached a nearby trainer: "Excuse me, sir, I'm curious. Why don't these elephants try to escape when it seems so easy for them to do so?"

The trainer smiled knowingly and replied, "Ah, when these elephants were small and vulnerable, we used that small rope to tie them up. At that age, it was strong enough to hold them in place. As they grew older and more powerful, they believed the same rope still had the power to restrain them. It's as if they carry the belief from their youth that they can't break free, so they never even attempt it."

When I first heard this story, I thought of Kyle and his equally ugly step-brother bullying me—I was like the little elephants. I was physically "restrained." I couldn't stop

13

attending school, I couldn't move away from the neighborhood, and I definitely couldn't simply ask them to stop bullying me. So, I had to live with it the best I could.

As I grew older, I grew stronger and could stop the physical bullying, but the opinions of others became the new rope holding me in place. Just as the elephants had been conditioned to believe they were stuck, so had I been conditioned to believe I wouldn't be accepted as I was. I had to mold myself into whatever opinion I valued most at the time. I began living in the captivity of other people's opinions. My rope: believing that to navigate this life successfully, I CAN'T BE MYSELF.

A seed was planted when Kyle punched me. Once the seed was planted, it only reaffirmed the limiting belief whenever I had a negative interaction with another person. Do you see how such a small event that happens to you as a kid can snowball into something that eventually shapes your behavior as an adult? Like being tied with a small rope, you become conditioned by hundreds of these experiences.

What is a limiting belief? A limiting belief is a belief or conviction about yourself, others, or the world that restricts your potential, personal growth, and the achievement of your goals. It is born from a moment or an event in which you make a conclusion about yourself or the world. You arrive at this conclusion by creating a story to justify the moment or event, and that story, often false and self-defeating in nature, is repeated in your head until you believe it to be true. And once it becomes true to you, it will shape how you interact with the world.

How do limiting beliefs plant themselves into your mind? Very subtly. Just like those bullies conditioned me to believe I couldn't and shouldn't be myself if I wanted to be accepted, you, too, have likely taken on some limiting beliefs. And you don't need to have been physically bullied. A negative comment about your freckles makes you believe you're ugly. A thoughtless joke by a friend, and you think you're stupid. A busy parent and you believe you're a burden. A distracted spouse and you feel you are not loved. A careless mistake, and you think you're unqualified. You were skipped over for the promotion and now believe you're not good enough. Your friends didn't invite you to a party, and you feel like a loser. It doesn't take much to form a limiting belief.

And do these only occur when you're a child or a teen? Nope. There will always be moments and opportunities for you to fall into the traps of limiting beliefs, even into your later years.

Think of some of your moments now; you'll realize these memories are often emotionally charged. A strong memory is created when you experience something that evokes a lot of negative emotion. Your brain creates these strong memories so that you can hopefully avoid experiencing that adverse event in the future. So the next time you want to raise your hand in class or a meeting, your brain screams, "WARNING, WARNING, you looked like an idiot the last time you asked a question; remember how bad that felt? So keep your hand down!"

And just like that, a limiting belief has robbed you of an opportunity.

Sometimes, it's even simpler, and we're like a radio tower picking up a broadcast signal, picking up limiting beliefs just by being around people who have them.

Maybe when you were young, your parents never went on vacation because, according to your dad, "Airplane tickets are expensive; we can't afford that." This may have been the truth for your parents, but you took the statement and made it a fact for you. And now, you are forty-five years old and haven't taken your dream vacation because "airplane tickets are expensive, I can't afford that."

For me, limiting beliefs, big and small, sabotaged my success, happiness, and path to purpose. They nearly robbed me of my biggest dreams.

Limiting beliefs are the root cause of anxiety, depression, and lack of self-confidence for millions of people. They keep you and me from pursuing our dreams. They make people eventually stop looking for answers to the question, "Why am I here?"

Let's take a look at a few more. Much like I began to believe that "I CAN'T BE MYSELF," the following story will show how quickly the world can make you think, "I'M NOT GOOD ENOUGH."

I began to live in the captivity of other people's opinions.

LIMITING BELIEF: "I'M NOT GOOD ENOUGH"

In the sixth grade, I thought I was a decent student. That is until my math teacher decided to try a little experiment. One day at the beginning of the third period, Mrs. Mateo had us split the room in two with our desks. Each side of the room had two rows of about twelve desks, divided by a significant gap in the middle of the room. Then she read a list of all the students in the class, and as she called out each name, she told us on which side of the room we would be sitting from now on.

It didn't take us long to realize that all the "smart" kids were coincidentally on one side of the room, and the struggling or "mediocre" students were on the other.

Guess which side of the room I sat on? Yep, the dumb side.

I need to state that Mrs. Mateo did not label the two sides of the room as "Smart" and "Dumb." Those were the labels we kids assigned. But we all understood what was happening. It's one thing to get a bad grade on a test; you keep it face down, and no one knows. But it's another thing to be publicly humiliated—especially in front of all the girls. Most of the girls were on the opposite side of the great desk divide from me. For a twelve-year-old kid entering puberty, it was not only embarrassing, it was downright traumatizing.

Mrs. Mateo's experiment was well-meaning. She split the room so the kids learning the lesson faster than others didn't have to be slowed down and the lagging students didn't get left behind. There was nothing wrong with her idea of teaching each group at their own pace.

But the public display and comparison of our math skills made half of us, who were decent students, feel dumb.

So, to save face, we did a terrible thing. All of us boys on the "dumb" side began clowning around. We hunched over, thumped our chests, grunted, and scratched our asses like cavemen. Poor Mrs. Mateo was horrified and started to cry as she apologized. She had us move all the desks back to the way before, and we were never split up again. I still feel pretty bad about making her cry.

I was generally a good student. I did my homework, studied hard for tests, and took pride in getting good grades. But I hated math and was lazy when studying it.

So, I always believed I was terrible at it because I didn't care, and if I wanted to, I could do better. This was probably the truth.

But after that day, I started to believe I was dumb when it came to math. My dad always told me I had to be good at math to get a good job, so being dumb at math meant I was not good enough for the success I hoped for.

Guess what happens when you believe you aren't good enough?

You don't go for the job you want. You don't go for the dreams you desire. You settle for something more accessible that suits a dumb, unqualified person like yourself. You pass on opportunities. You don't try new things to protect yourself from failing at them and looking stupid again, confirming that you are not good enough.

And just like that, another limiting belief is born.

LIMITING BELIEF: "I'M NOT WORTHY OF WHAT I DESIRE"

When I was sixteen, I had a massive crush on a girl from another school. I didn't get to see her during the week since we lived on different sides of town, and I hadn't passed my driver's test yet. But we texted daily for hours and hung out a lot with mutual friends on the weekends.

Though I was too scared to ask her on a date, I was positive this was the girl I would one day marry.

One day, I discovered my number was saved in her phone as "My Crush," I was thrilled to know the feelings were mutual. In my mind, there was no way this could turn out other than happily ever after.

Unfortunately for me, she didn't have the same imagination for our perfect future, or maybe she met someone else. One day, I sent my most clever and flirtatious text. She replied by telling me I was too short for her and then ghosted me altogether.

That one hurt. But I couldn't argue with her. I was only 5'3" and didn't hit my growth spurt until my junior year. While her rejection made me self-conscious about my height, I comforted myself, knowing I would still grow a little. I figured she just used my height as an excuse to get me to leave her alone. I began to wonder what else was wrong with me and became very insecure about the way I looked. Or maybe it was my personality; perhaps I was too awkward, and my texts weren't as clever as I thought. Maybe it was the off-brand clothes I wore.

I started to overthink everything. Her friends didn't like me, or maybe that tall new kid caught her eye. Perhaps she hated my voice, my hair, my sense of humor—and that's why she suddenly cut me off.

I developed the limiting belief that I couldn't just go for

what I wanted in life. I believed there would always be someone more deserving of whatever I wanted, so who was I to go for it? I developed a bad attitude toward girls. I thought it was cool to be rude and emotionless and pretend I didn't care about someone whenever they showed interest in me. This way, I would never be hurt again. And when a tall, handsome guy would come around our friend group, I said nasty, untrue things behind his back. This way, I could hide my jealousy.

Do you see how ugly you and I can act when we feel unworthy and fear rejection? Do you see how it will interfere with moving toward our desires? It took me years into adulthood to pinpoint the basis for many of my behaviors.

The final limiting belief I want to share for now will remind you how quickly the world can teach you to *keep your brilliant ideas to yourself.*

LIMITING BELIEF: "I DON'T HAVE WHAT IT TAKES"

It was my first semester in community college. According to my counselor, I needed a communications credit to get my associate's degree in computer science. Because I was late picking my classes, all the other easy communication classes were at capacity, so I was stuck taking the public speaking class. I was mad. Why did I need to learn public speaking to work with computers!?

Our first assignment was to pick any topic we wanted and write a three-minute speech about it with an introduction, a few main points, and a conclusion. To play it safe, I picked an easy topic. I chose to talk about the impact of community sports. It should have been a breeze, right? Wrong.

When the presentation day came, I was beyond nervous. I was paralyzed with fear. My throat was dry. My hands wouldn't stop shaking. And for some reason, my thighs felt like Jell-O. I could barely stand.

Remember, by this time, I had learned to lay low and keep my ideas to myself throughout my middle and high school career. I did not fit in with my classmates and was about to prove beyond a shadow of a doubt that I didn't belong. As I started my speech, my voice trembled. My vision blurred. I may have gotten through my introduction and was on to my first main point when my mind decided to leave the room. I completely forgot what I was trying to say. I forgot what I had just said before and had no idea what I was supposed to say next.

I stared at all the students in the class, and they stared back at me. My face burned, I could even feel my ears turn red, and I walked straight to my desk in the middle of my speech. I grabbed my backpack and left the classroom.

The next day, I went to my counselor, dropped the class, and swore I would never step on a stage again.

Today, I speak to large groups, sometimes in arenas with thousands of people. And we'll get to how the heck that happened in later chapters. But after that speech class fail, I gained another limiting belief. I believed I was not cut out to do big things with my life. I had run away. How could I succeed if I quit at every obstacle and fear I faced? My dwindling confidence took another hit, another pathetic failure. More proof that I was never meant to be among the brightest or the bravest.

Remember the formula? A negative event is experienced, a story is created, and a conclusion is made. Then, the story is repeated until it becomes the truth, and a limiting belief is born.

That one decision to run away made me a quitter in other areas of my life, too. I quit at the first sign of discomfort. That same semester, the minute things got hard at a shipping warehouse I worked at, I quit. I quit volunteering for a non-profit serving old people because I felt awkward talking to them. I quit a business my brothers and I tried to start because it wasn't working as we had hoped. I was a pinball, bouncing from job to job, idea to idea, without ever following through on anything or sticking to it long enough to succeed. Not because I was incapable but because I had discovered an easy way to avoid the failure I believed was inevitable.

I'm here to tell you it's IMPOSSIBLE to be confident when you see a quitter every time you look in the mirror.

Is this a belief that limits a person? Absolutely!

If you don't recognize and identify your limiting beliefs, then pursuing your dreams, discovering your purpose, and doing extraordinary things in this world will be nearly impossible. How can you have an open heart to love others if you carry self-hate? How can you reach your greatest potential and inspire others to do the same if you are full of self-doubts? What can you achieve if you keep sabotaging your own success because you quit at every sign of adversity?

Success requires discipline, confidence, constant self-improvement, awareness, love, respect, leadership skills, persistence, a positive mind, and positive habits. Limiting beliefs are the killers of all those things.

Have you ever been to a wedding, party, or maybe a high school dance, and everyone was on the dance floor, but you remained glued to your seat? You wanted to get out there, but you were afraid of looking foolish and kept hesitating, trying to convince yourself you could find the right moment to jump in, and then the night was over. And you've regretted it ever since, wishing you had that opportunity back?

Well, guess what, my friend? Life is that dance. But unlike that party that came and went, you're still here, and it's not over, so you still have time to get off the seat and jump into the dance!

In the next chapter, I will share *Big Idea #1,* which you can use to identify and destroy limiting beliefs so you can groove toward your purpose and your biggest dreams.

Are you ready for the first big idea? I'll see you in Chapter Three.

Three

Big Idea #1: BELIEVE IN YOURSELF

You become whatever you believe about yourself

There once were two brothers who were raised by an abusive alcoholic father. One brother became a successful entrepreneur. He was happily married, had a great relationship with his children, lived in a beautiful home, and lived a happy life. His brother, however, became an alcoholic. He eventually divorced his wife and verbally abused his children until they no longer wanted to see him, and after years of financial struggle, he became homeless.

One day, while he sat in an alley, the struggling brother was asked, "How did you get to this place in your life?" He answered, "I am who I am today because my father was an abusive, worthless alcoholic."

His successful brother was asked the same question: "How did you get to this place in your life?" His answer was identical to that of his struggling brother. "I am who I am today because my father was an abusive, worthless alcoholic."

Both experienced the same circumstance, but each

developed a different belief around it. One brother believed that since an abusive alcoholic father raised him, he was destined for the same life. His limiting beliefs caused him to repeat the same vicious cycle he was once a victim of. He believed he came from nothing and was destined for nothing, so he became nothing.

The other brother, however, developed an empowering belief instead of a limiting belief around the same adverse circumstance. He believed he came from nothing and there was nowhere to go but up, so he became something.

What a wild idea. Imagine if more people understood that they shape their lives with their beliefs. Imagine if more people used their unfavorable circumstances as a launch pad instead of allowing them to be quicksand.

That's what *Big Idea #1* is all about. It's about changing your limiting beliefs to become who you want to be.

What do you believe about yourself, my friend?

Let me ask that another way…

Who would you blame if you don't reach your full potential in life, your parents or your difficult upbringing? Your school? Your job? Your lack of opportunity? The friends you have or the friends you lack? The way you look? Maybe it's the way your mind works? The neighborhood you grew up in? The country you were born in? The circumstances you were born into? Those pesky Commies?

If you said yes to any of these, it looks like you have a little work to do in this chapter. Though all of these factors certainly affect how we perceive the world and can create many challenges to overcome, the *real* dream killers are our limiting beliefs.

There is nothing you can't overcome in life as long as you believe you can. I know people who were blessed with everything and squandered their lives away, and I have friends who had the entire world stacked against them and still succeeded.

You become whatever you believe about yourself. So, if you believe you can't succeed and achieve your dreams, you won't. If you believe you can, you will. I am sure you've heard this idea in one form or another, but I want you to understand the magnitude of it.

Here lies the beginning of your success and purpose, and here lies the demise of it. It all starts with you. In your mind, you give birth to your dreams, and in your mind, you destroy them.

If you believe you can't, you won't. If you believe you can, you will!

Your mind is powerful beyond comprehension. With your thoughts and beliefs, you attract to yourself whatever you think about most. This is why I am stressing this idea so much. Watch your thoughts because they become beliefs. Watch your beliefs because they become actions. Watch your actions because they determine your life!

So, if you and I become whatever we believe about ourselves, it's time to turn some limiting beliefs into empowering beliefs so they work for us instead of against us.

CHANGE LIMITING BELIEFS TO EMPOWERING BELIEFS

Take a few minutes right now to close your eyes and imagine that you can fly back in time to different moments in your life, just like I had to do when I shared those four stories from my youth that created limiting beliefs in me.

"Fly" back—whether it's a decade, a few years, or only a few weeks—to find a moment where you felt neglected, dumb, unwanted, unloved, left out, or unqualified.

Did someone mock your idea?

Did someone reject you?

Were you bullied or excluded from a group of friends?

Were you judged?

Did you make a mistake?

Did you fail at something?

Did you break someone's trust?

Did you make a bad investment?

Whatever it was, you might not have realized it then, but after each of those moments, a story unfolded in your mind that you began to repeat.

Now let me ask you this: Did you hear forgiving, motivating, and encouraging stories that made you want to try again or be better? Did you say to yourself, *"It's okay, I'll do better next time."* Or *"It's okay, I may have misunderstood that person's comment."*

If you're like most people, you did not. In fact, you likely repeated stories that obliterated your self-confidence.

"I probably looked like an idiot."

"I'm pathetic."

"I'm useless."

"I'm worthless."

"I'm a fraud."

"I don't belong here."

"I'm a nobody."

"I don't have the same opportunities."

"I don't have what it takes."

"I'm lazy; I've always been that way."

"I'm just like my mom."

"I'm just like my dad."

I can go on forever because I've said all these things to myself—and thousands more.

Whether it's a story of guilt, shame, or rejection, these stories eventually turn into beliefs, as discussed in the previous chapter. One moment sets them in motion, and that's all it takes for the brain to put them on repeat like a radio station overplaying the latest Taylor Swift song. They never stop playing in the background; the more they play, the deeper into your subconscious mind they bury themselves.

What started as a negative observation turns into a label, which turns into a story, then a belief, and then it dictates your actions and eventually shapes your future. These stories must be stopped, changed, and weaponized to work for you instead of against you.

I will give you a few tools you can use to begin changing

those beliefs into empowering beliefs to provide you with confidence instead of self-doubt, hope instead of despair, and positive, empowering thoughts instead of negative and anxious ones.

STOP ACCEPTING THE LABELS

Before you put too much energy into uprooting existing limiting beliefs, you must first stop the growth of new limiting beliefs. Otherwise, you will never stay ahead of the cycle. I have had many frustrating conversations with people who want help unraveling their past but won't consider how their current mindset might be responsible for their inability to have breakthroughs and keeps them in the same cycle.

Agree with me now to no longer accept negative labels about yourself.

If you have difficulty making friends, a label you've probably accepted is that you're awkward. Or you're not attractive to people. Or you're unlikable. You didn't invent these labels; you learned them over time. Perhaps you've been a part of some gossip, and someone said something like, "That girl is so cringe!" And you instantly began to wonder if you, too, have ever been "cringe." Now you're replaying your last ten social gatherings and remembering your cringe-worthy moments, and suddenly, you discovered a new label to use against yourself:

"Cringe."

Of course, everybody won't like you and me, nor should we try to be liked by everybody. I'm sure thousands of people will find me dull, awkward, unlikable, or "cringe," but that doesn't define me as a motivational speaker, author, or human. If someone doesn't like me, that's okay. I don't accept the labels nor try to change their opinion of me. I let them have it. It's in the attempt to be liked by everybody that we lose ourselves.

So, instead of accepting a negative label about yourself, ask yourself, "Are these people I'm trying so hard to impress even people I would enjoy being around all the time?" The chances are you won't. Because fitting in with people who have the same interests and goals as you will be effortless. If you find yourself trying too hard to fit in, you might be trying to fit into the wrong herd.

Yes, having great self-awareness is essential. We all have room to improve in some areas of our lives. For example, if you tend to interrupt people in conversations, you might want to be mindful of that. But growth can happen without attaching labels.

Be genuine, and you will attract the right people into your life. There is no need to analyze, rationalize, and obsess over your rejections; there is no need for a label.

Remember, nothing has any meaning except the meaning you assign to it. So, stop giving a negative label to every experience. Put the label maker away. The problem with you and me is that our brain somehow manages to find the worst-case scenario in everything in a universe of infinite possibilities. You can't blame your brain; its job is to keep you safe. It's always on the alert for danger.

So, it is up to us to define what is dangerous and what isn't so that we can stop living in fear. We need to learn to see the negative labels and stories for their lies and not let our imagination get away from us.

Your dreams are waiting for the version of you that shows up in life with no labels attached.

It's in the attempt to be liked by everybody that we lose ourselves.

CHANGE THE STORY

When my crush rejected me, I accepted the label "I am unworthy." Because I couldn't understand why I was rejected, I concluded that she found someone better than me. I told myself there would always be someone taller, better looking, funnier, and more muscular with more money than me. This story played in my head whenever I started to like another girl. So, to protect myself from heartbreak, I avoided relationships. Had I told myself a different story and assigned a different meaning to the rejection instead of accepting the label, I would not have the limiting belief that I needed to avoid relationships to be "safe."

What if I would have told myself that through that rejection, I was being guided to someone special I haven't even met yet? That there was more in store for me, so this wasn't the right time and person? What if I had accepted the rejection as a sign that I needed to grow first and not place all my identity and self-worth into the hands of another person?

Without that rejection, I may have never met my wife. And that would have been a tragedy. Of course, it is easy to look back and make these observations now that years have passed, but that's what makes this concept so important. If you learn to change the story *now,* you can save yourself from years of self-sabotage.

Remember, if you stop telling yourself negative stories, you will soon realize that everything works for your good! You'll see that every bully, rejection, setback, and failure only makes you a stronger, wiser, more open-minded, resilient, and loving extraordinary person.

It takes practice. It's difficult to tell yourself a positive, empowering story when your brain does everything possible to keep you focused on the negative. For every 30 positive book reviews I get on Amazon.com, I get one negative one. And guess which one affects me the most? Yep, the negative review is the one I obsess about. I catch myself saying, "Maybe all the good reviews are from people just being nice, and this one mean guy is the only one brave enough to speak the truth about my book."

So you see, even now, I battle with the stories in my head. But these days, I immediately change the story because I've made myself aware of negativity and know how crucial it is to my success to cut out the negative stories. If I let them take hold of my mind, they can stop me from ever writing anything again.

Early in my speaking career, I was hired by an organization to speak to a group of city mayors and planners from all over Oregon. I was scared to death. The audience was a room full of influential people who were twice my age. How was I supposed to inspire people who were more experienced and successful than me? What could I say to them? I was nearly paralyzed by imposter syndrome and the belief that I did not belong there.

So what did I do? I put these same tools that I'm sharing with you to practice. I started telling myself a different story! I found a quiet place in the convention center, closed my eyes, took a few deep breaths, and began to go back through all of my successful speaking engagements. I reminded myself that I did belong there because I had something to say. I reminded myself that I had been hand-picked by the event organizers from a list of other fantastic speakers. I reminded myself that I've always delivered a successful speech, no matter how nervous I was before speaking. I reminded myself of the people who constantly lined up after I presented to meet me and thank me for coming to speak. I reminded myself that someone in this room needed encouragement, and if I didn't deliver my message, they might give up on themselves. I reminded myself of the high school girl after an assembly and the businessman at a conference who told me my words saved them from suicide.

After only a few minutes of going over my wins in my mind, I was fired up and ready to run on to the stage; that is precisely what I did. Changing the story completely changed my attitude, and afterward, people lined up to thank me for my speech and take photos with me.

The key is to train your mind to work for you instead of against you. I could take control of the narrative in my mind in that crisis moment only because it was already something I had made a habit of doing. Facing fear was not uncommon for me anymore; I knew what I needed to do to be ready. But if it hadn't already been my practice, I might have lost the battle to the fear, and who knows if I would have ever taken the stage.

Train for the race before you are in it. Don't wait until something negative happens to put positive thinking into practice. If you stay ready, you don't have to get ready. The time to create powerful positive thinking routines and habits is in a time of peace when taking control of your thoughts is easy. Not in a crisis moment. The navy seals say this, "We don't rise to the level of our expectations, we fall to the level of our training."

Every morning, take a few minutes to open up a journal and put your pen to work. Remind yourself of past wins, compliments, and the words of encouragement you have received along the way. Remind yourself of your destination. Remind yourself of who you are and what you are capable of, and see how your perspective will change instantly. When you fix your heart and mind on what is good and uplifting, negativity flees. *That's* how you change your story.

Train for the race before you are in it.

EXPAND, VISUALIZE, AND BELIEVE

Understand this, my friend: You can't become what you can't wrap your head around. When believing in what's possible, it has to be out with the old and in with the new. Your view of the world must first *expand*. You've got to see what's possible, then you can believe it's possible for you. If you can expand your mind, you'll shrink the doubts about what it will take to achieve your dreams. And once you realize just how far you can go, you'll never think small again.

Do you know why so many people think and play small in

life? Because they are surrounded by people who think and play small. It's hard to believe in what's possible when all they see is mediocrity. Yes, they can have an imagination and might see other people doing extraordinary things, but there is no room for belief in their minds.

A boy in the slums of India has undoubtedly seen private jets flying overhead, but if he doesn't believe it's possible for *him,* the power of his mind is never activated. He might as well be looking at a UFO. No direct line of possibility leads him from the slums to the jet.

But what if the boy has a cousin who has a friend who learned how to code on YouTube? Maybe that friend left the slums to find a job in the city, and sometime later, his ability to code landed him an opportunity to create software. Eventually, he sells that software, which gives him enough money to buy a private jet.

Suddenly, the little boy in the slums has a different perspective; his mind has been expanded. He's seen the direct link between the slums and the jet. He's seen what's possible for someone who is just like him. Poverty is no longer something he has to be destined for; indeed, there is another possibility.

Whether he believes he can achieve this and takes action is another story—I'll get to that part shortly. Still, now you can see how necessary it is to surround yourself with more people, stories, and experiences of greater possibility. You and I have enough negative thinkers around us; it's time to find ways to expand our thinking.

Reading a book, listening to a podcast, watching a movie, listening to a speaker, surrounding yourself with successful people, going to a networking event, traveling to another country, or chatting with a stranger are just a few of the ways to open your mind to what's possible and to get ideas beyond what you could ever get from your friends and co-workers and your comfort zone. I challenge you to find ways to expand your mind daily.

So, how do you believe that something is not only possible but possible for *you?* How does the boy in India believe that a private jet is possible for him?

Good question. When you give yourself the permission to say, "I want that! How do I get it?" Be ready because you've just opened the door to infinite possibilities with that line of thinking. I'm not trying to sell you the idea that money will fall from the sky if you sit and dream big enough. That wasn't the purpose of using the example of a private jet. The purpose of that example is to show you that there will always be a big gap between you and your dreams, and sometimes, the only bridge between where you are and where you want to go is built solely on belief.

Your mind, which has no limitations to what it can conceive and believe if given the freedom to, will work on finding a way to bend the universe in your favor and get it for you. You only need to grant it permission to do so.

It's when you say, "That's impossible for me," that you close the door to miracles.

The great inventor Thomas Edison mastered letting his mind perform miracles for him. When he'd run into an invention he couldn't find a solution for, he would nap on his workbench in the shop. He would often leap from his bench and race back to work because the answer had come to him in his sleep. He did not place restrictions on what was possible; instead, he understood the power of his mind and let his subconscious get to work. You've got something powerful between your two ears. Let it work for you, not against you.

Edison also understood that though powerful and limitless, the mind also needs direction. As the saying goes, "Idle hands are the devil's workshop." If not given a worthwhile assignment, an idle mind will undoubtedly find something to occupy itself with, and it won't be anything good, positive, or brilliant. You can take my word for it. Unmonitored, our thoughts tend to drift to the negative.

Enter the *Reticular Activating System* (RAS). This network of neurons in your brain stem filters through information and brings to your conscious awareness anything you deem important to you. Imagine you're at a noisy party with loud conversation, music playing, and other distracting sounds. Your brain can't possibly process every single sound equally; you'd be overwhelmed. This is where the RAS comes into play.

The RAS selectively filters out the less important information (like the background chatter or the hum of the refrigerator) and allows the more critical information to reach your conscious awareness. For instance, if someone at the party calls your name or mentions your favorite song, your RAS snaps into action and alerts you, and you perk your ears up. It helps you focus on what's essential while ignoring the constant background noise.

Whether positive or negative, what you deem important eventually enters your subconscious mind, and your RAS keeps you alert to what's important. If drama and gossip are important, I promise that you won't miss it if anyone around you is dishing the latest gossip. Likewise, if you dream of opening a coffee shop, I promise you won't scroll past an ad on Facebook about roasting beans.

This is why two people can look at the same circumstance and interpret it so differently. One will see it as an opportunity because he has programmed his mind to spot anything that might look like an opportunity to get closer to his goal, and the other will see it as a setback because his mind has been programmed to focus on the negative.

If you've watched Top Gun, you've seen a radar-guided missile in action. Once a radar-guided missile locks on its target, no matter how or where the target moves, the missile can continue to track it and hit it. Your mind is like a radar-guided missile; it can only hit its target once it has a specific target to track using RAS. Even if the target moves, your mind—like the missile—will continue to calculate, adjust, course correct, and track it down! But without a clear and specific target, the missile goes rogue. And so will your mind.

If you don't intentionally define what is important to you, your mind will track down your worst fears and insecurities instead of your goals.

Here is where the practice of *visualization* comes in.

Visualization will be one of your greatest tools for successfully turning limiting beliefs into empowering ones. Through visualization, you consistently and intentionally program your mind with information that is important to you so that your RAS can get to work.

You don't need to map out every step of the way. You don't need to know how your "invention" will come together; you just need to give direction to what you want and how it feels to be there. If you can find time every day to sit in silence, close your eyes, and picture yourself doing and being exactly who you want to be, your mind will see this clear picture as a reality.

Remember, to the mind, it's all real. Whatever we imagine, whether positive or negative, the mind believes it to be so. So why not get your mind to think that this future version of you is already in existence? Why not get your mind to lock on the target of your dreams?

Put yourself into the perfect day of a future you. What are you seeing? Smelling? Hearing? What music do you have on in what car, where are you heading, and in what city or country? What are you wearing? Are you going to a meeting to sign a contract with a music label? Or sign a book deal? Are you meeting a realtor to get the keys to your dream house on your dream property? What does your body feel like? Can you feel the abs when you flex? Can you go for a five-mile jog without being exhausted? Whose hand are you holding? Imagine the joy in your heart as you are holding it. Is there a dog in the picture? Be clear and specific.

And most importantly, *feel!* Just like emotionally charged negative events in your life caused your brain to hold on to those negative memories and relive them over and over again, making you physically feel sick to your stomach, in the same way, your positive visualizations will emotionally charge your body to feel the joy, excitement, gratitude, and enthusiasm as if you have already achieved those things.

Practice this visualization regularly, ideally as part of a daily routine. It won't come easy at first. New habits rarely do. Be intentional, and be consistent. The more consistently you combine your mental images with strong positive emotions, the more your creativity and imagination flourish and the more impact it will have on your subconscious mind.

When you hold a positive image of yourself in your mind, your limiting beliefs have no basis to exist. Your mind is forced to create a new story of how you became the greatest *you* because that's how your mind works. Instead of justifying the story of why you aren't capable, worthy, or qualified, your mind will justify why you are. This is the power of visualization.

Napoleon Hill, author of *Think and Grow Rich,* called this the principle of *autosuggestion.* When thoughts in the mind become mixed with strong emotions in the body, they immediately enter the subconscious mind.

Knowing this, keep a positive image of yourself and your future in mind. And soon, your Reticular Activating System (RAS) will ensure you experience more of whatever you see.

You will begin to ***believe!***

A single book changed my life through this powerful process before I even understood the science behind it.

My family came to America in 1990. We left what was back then the former Soviet Union, or Communist Russia. My parents carried a few bags of belongings and seven children in their arms. At the time, I was two years old and gave my dad hell the entire trip by throwing a fit any time he tried to set me down or hand me to one of my siblings. Somehow, they got us all to Austin, Texas, even with all the layovers and sleepless nights in airports. And then, three months later, we piled into a big yellow Penske truck and moved to the Pacific Northwest.

Mom and Dad did not have a spare dollar in their pockets

when we arrived in America. Yet, despite the difficulties they faced trying to make ends meet in a foreign country, they somehow managed to feed us, keep a roof over our heads, and eventually succeed in America as immigrants.

Growing up, my parents saved every possible penny to make that happen. We never ate out in restaurants or went on vacations and rarely got Christmas presents. And for all that, I am beyond grateful to them because I got to witness them make the impossible possible while keeping true to their faith and values and being present for their children. I wouldn't trade that experience for any toys, vacations, or material things in the world.

I learned about hard work, sacrifice, patience, persistence, faith, love, and family—all those priceless things many people take for granted or abandon for instant gratification.

But as I was growing and trying to discover my place in this world, my mind was pretty closed off to what was possible because I understood that I couldn't survive without money. And as far as I could tell, the best way to get money was by getting a job and exchanging hard-working hours for dollars. It was pretty straightforward. That was the quickest route to success.

On TV, I saw people acting in movies or playing professional sports, writing books, inventing machines, writing music, or creating their brands, and all those things intrigued me but didn't feel like options for me.

Once, a children's book author came to our school for the Scholastic Book Fair, and I shook her hand. I couldn't believe I met a real author! But because no one in my immediate surroundings was doing any of those things, and I never had a cousin who had a friend who became successful from writing books, it never registered in my mind that it was a possibility for *me*.

And so even though I had a great imagination and dreamed about how cool it would be to be an author, invent something, or play quarterback for the Seattle Seahawks, my RAS was shut off to those things. I believed it was just for people on TV, lucky extraordinary people. Not for people like me. The power of my mind was never activated. I lacked belief. I was a guided missile with no target—certainly moving and possessing incredible energy, but never locked on anything extraordinary.

After high school, I had to be "realistic" about my career choices. I went to community college because everyone I knew was going to community college. I picked a random career I was not passionate about because everyone said it was good and safe. And eventually, I got a job and had to drive to work in traffic along with everybody, come home in traffic with everybody, and ultimately be miserable along with everybody. I hit the targets I locked on; the problem was I locked on the wrong targets.

Do you see how even a kid with a great imagination could be limited by his immediate surroundings? Maybe you've been there too. Perhaps you're reading this book and you sense a feeling rising up. You become filled with possibility—and then you set the book down on your torn couch in your old house that needs new plumbing, and again, reality sets in and drowns out the possibility. Visualization is a powerful tool, but it needs to be practiced daily to keep the images of "reality" from killing the ideas of "possibility" until you are well on the way to your goals.

What are your immediate surroundings?

What does your "herd" look like?

Who do you spend the most time with?

What are your friends doing?

What topics are they discussing?

Do they support your dreams?

What are their dreams?

Are they striving towards those dreams?

Or do you spend time discussing drama, gossip, and useless things?

Do victims, blamers, and complainers surround you?

Remember, you become like the people you spend the most time with because even though you have a great imagination, through the principle of autosuggestion, you'll believe in only what you continually see. Whatever you take in most will shape you. The word "inspiration" comes from the Latin word "inspiratus," which essentially means "breathe into." Be careful of what you continually breathe in.

Along with the practice of visualization, keep yourself in a positive environment as much as possible so your surroundings don't constantly contradict your dreams.

Positive thoughts combined with strong emotions give birth to new beliefs.

So, how did a book change my life? I'm glad you reminded me. The book was called *A Better Way to Live* by Og Mandino. In the book, Mandino writes about his life after coming home from the Second World War, the addictions, poverty, and suicide attempts he overcame, and eventually, how he became an author and motivational speaker.

It was just what I needed at a time when I was depressed and miserable at my corporate job right out of college, and it became like a moment of re-birth for me. As I studied his book and applied the principles he taught, the thought of inspiring people through writing and speaking struck me as a genuinely fulfilling career. But it never occurred to me that it was something I could pursue.

I thought it was a job reserved for successful athletes, entrepreneurs, or movie stars, people who had earned the right to encourage the rest of us... until I finished Mr. Mandino's book, and then something changed. It was like a switch was suddenly flipped on in my mind, and a new dream crept into my most secret thoughts—maybe I could do it too! Remember the section on *expanding* your mind and giving yourself permission to ask for what you want?

Og Mandino used to be a homeless, suicidal drunkard. If he could turn his life around so drastically to become an author and motivational speaker, what was stopping me from pursuing my dream?

What exactly was it, then, that disqualified me?

I didn't want this to be another idea that fizzled with time, so I read all of his books to stay inspired. I watched old, blurry video recordings of his speeches and started watching hundreds of other speakers. I sketched myself speaking to crowds on sticky notes and stuck them on my cubicle walls and car dashboard. I imagined walking up on stage, visualized telling different personal stories to audiences, and practiced extracting examples and inspirational points from those stories. I often would visualize with such detail that I would feel butterflies in my stomach as if I was about to walk out on stage and speak to an audience. And my belief only grew. Remember the part about **visualizing** with emotion to change your **beliefs?**

Even though I was still working at that job, my obsessive visualizing, drawing, and practicing caused me to believe in the dream so much that in my mind, through the principle of autosuggestion, I was already an author and a motivational speaker long before I typed the first chapter of my first book or stepped on an actual stage. I even started having dreams of myself speaking on stage, which meant the intentional practice of visualization was taking effect, and my conscious imagination had entered my subconscious mind!

Again, positive thoughts combined with strong emotions give birth to new beliefs, and soon, *"According to your faith, it will be done unto you."*

"According to your faith, it will be done unto you."

AFFIRMATIONS

In middle school, my mom stopped me at the front door before I went to the bus stop every morning. She placed both palms on my face, kissed my forehead, and said,

"You are talented, Michael. You are smart, you are strong, you are healthy, you are blessed, and you are capable."

Back then, I didn't understand what she was doing. I knew I was strong, and I knew I was healthy. But you see, my friend, my mom wasn't stating the obvious or trying to give me a false sense of confidence. She was speaking that *into* my life. She was speaking that over me. She was seeing what was possible for me before I could. She was planting seeds into my subconscious mind. She knew she could not be there to protect her son from the mistakes he would make, from the bullies he would face, or from the words and opinions of others. But she understood the power of words, and she used her words to combat the negativity I would inevitably face.

Along with expanding your mind, visualizing, and believing, continue to apply the principle of autosuggestion by affirming the truth to yourself. Affirmations are powerful. Affirmations are the antidote to limiting beliefs. Affirmations give you the power to detect and eliminate negative labels and change the story in your head. They allow you to see something better, even if it's not happening yet. Use affirmations to speak your future into existence.

When I wanted to change my story, I suddenly understood what my mom was doing when I was a child, and those seeds she planted many years ago started to bear fruit. These days, I talk to myself just like my mom spoke to me when I was a child. Whenever a limiting belief creeps up on me, I remind myself that I am talented, I am capable, I am qualified, I am worthy, I am appreciated, I am loved, I belong, and I can do anything I put my mind to. If you're thinking this sounds cheesy, think again. Words are powerful. There is nothing cheesy about setting yourself up for success. There is nothing cheesy about planting seeds of belief into the mind of your children, friends, family, or people you lead.

In my first novel, *The Mount of Olives: 11 Declarations to an Extraordinary Life,* I wrote about a Roman orphan boy on a journey of self-discovery. In the story, he learns eleven life-changing principles from a wealthy Arabian merchant as he runs away from Rome to Jerusalem. These are principles I still teach in my speeches. If you have heard me speak before or have read the book, you will know that the first principle is, ***"Words spoken set life in motion."***

I made this the first principle because everything starts with words. Your words shape your thoughts. Your words shape your stories. Your words shape your beliefs. Your words even have the power to shape other people's beliefs. Telling someone they are worthless can ruin their week, and telling someone you believe in them can save their life.

I mentioned earlier that I've had people come up to me after speeches and tell me they had been contemplating suicide, but something I said in the speech made them believe there was more in store for them. I also once received an email from a gentleman who had read my book, The Mount of Olives. His career had fallen apart and his wife had left him. It was nearing Christmastime, and because he was so alone, he had planned to kill himself. He told me my words in the book gave him a new life.

From teens to elders, people are struggling out there. You never know what someone is going through because most people won't show it on the outside. Your words can save someone else's life; your words can save your own life.

The mind is a wonderful thing; it can take you where you want to go or keep you a prisoner. It all depends on you.

***

My friend, do you see how much of your success depends entirely on what you believe about yourself?

Don't get me wrong—I understand that you may be dealing with circumstances in your life that were thrust upon you. I'm not saying that you brought troubles and obstacles into your life alone. After speaking to students and business professionals across the country, I know that at any given moment, in every audience, in every school, in every country, there are people who pretend they are okay on the outside but are falling apart on the inside. I don't intend to make light of life's difficulties by saying that your success depends entirely on you.

I am saying, though, that you can't let life's circumstances and obstacles and failures beat your dreams out of you by making you believe you are somehow not worthy of them. Don't let negativity win. *Big Idea #1* is all about reminding you that **you become whatever you believe about yourself,** so it's time to BELIEVE IN YOURSELF.

If you use the tools in this chapter to change your thoughts and expand your mind, any negativity you face will only make you stronger, tougher, more resilient, and more brilliant.

If you can see it, you can believe it, and you will become it.

The summer after my eighth-grade graduation, my family moved out of Washougal, Washington, the little town I had lived in from kindergarten through middle school. I did not get to go to high school with all of my friends. But even though I did not graduate from Washougal

High School, I got the opportunity to go back for the ten-year high school reunion. I wanted to see all the friends I hadn't seen since that summer before we moved away fourteen years earlier. These are the same kids I have gone to school with since kindergarten, so I was so excited to reconnect with them.

After many hugs, high-fives, and greetings, I noticed a table near the back of the room with candles and three framed portraits. As I walked up, I recognized each one. I had sat next to each of these kids in one class or another many times over the years. One of the boys was my next-door neighbor. All three had committed suicide.

I thought about where our lives had taken us. The paths that we chose, the difficulties that each of us faced, and the choices we made that shaped our lives in all those years that led to that reunion. I wondered where, along the way, these three classmates of mine, who were still innocent middle school kids when I moved away, lost the battle with their thoughts. I wondered how the world had led them to believe it was better for them to take their own life than to be here.

Standing before those portraits, I muttered, "*This* is why I'm here." I was reminded again why I wanted to write inspirational books and become a motivational speaker. People are desperate for encouragement, and there is not enough of it out there.

My friend, I believe in you. Now, it's time for you to

believe in yourself.

I'll see you in chapter four for Big Idea #2.

Four

Big Idea #2: BELIEVE IN OTHERS

Your purpose is to create a positive ripple in the world

I am one of thirteen siblings. Yep, I know that's a lot. Same mom and dad, too. I always get quite the reaction from audiences when I share that from the stage. I have five sisters and seven brothers, and I have no idea what my parents were thinking having so many children, but I am grateful for every one of my siblings.

Every Christmas, our family rents a big cabin, sometimes two, to fit all the siblings plus wives, husbands, nieces, and nephews. All of my brothers are married now, and our wives recently decided to pull a prank on the eight of us during our annual family gathering.

Before dinner one of the evenings at the cabin, my wife surprised me with a new long-sleeved flannel. As I was putting it on, I heard a commotion downstairs in the living room, and when I walked out, I saw that all of my brothers were wearing the same blue flannel I had on. They were trying to sort out how this could have happened, and suddenly, we all realized what the girls had done.

We pointed at each other, high-fived, laughed, huddled like a football team, and spun in a circle. Then we line danced and did high kicks in our matching shirts. We thought it was the best thing ever. My sister-in-law recorded the reactions and posted the video to TikTok. By the following day, the video had gained millions of views on her account. She was getting messages from entertainment sites asking permission to repost the video.

If you search "8 brothers - matching shirt prank," you will find videos from Newsweek, The New York Post, The Epoch Times, and all of the Instagram, Facebook, and TikTok entertainment pages that made the video go viral. I recently did a quick search—the video had collectively garnered over eighty million views.

The reaction blew us away. To us, this was nothing new or viral-worthy. This was how my family gatherings typically go… loud, chaotic, and with an endless amount of dancing. The matching shirts just sparked the inevitable. My brothers and I are close, and we love to clown around as it is, but give us matching outfits, and the party doesn't stop. We've been doing it since we were in diapers, and I'm sure we'll be doing it until we are in adult diapers, too. But if you take some time to read the comments on the viral videos, you will understand why the prank and subsequent reaction had such a significant impact on the social media world.

The number of comments that mentioned our bond as brothers was overwhelming. People commented about the love they could see between us and how incredible it would have been to grow up in our household. They wanted to know our story, they wanted to know about our parents, they wanted to know our names, what order we were born in, and what the age difference was between us all. They were inspired by what we had.

And what is it that we have that was displayed in our reaction to the prank? I believe people saw an unbreakable bond, community, friendship, love, connection, relationship, safety, care, empathy, kindness, support, camaraderie, and most definitely joy.

In today's digitally "connected" world, people report being lonelier than ever. In many ways and for many reasons, we have been neglecting one of our most essential life forces, human connection. And I'm sorry to my dog and cat people; your furry friends cannot replace your need for human connection.

These days, we can work from home, stream millions of hours of entertainment from our couch, and have food delivered right to our door without ever speaking with a single person face to face. We believe isolation is convenient and that being social has too many risks. New housing developments pack our houses like sardines, people constantly surround us, and we still refuse to meet our neighbors even though we barbeque ten feet away in our little yards divided by tall fences.

Going to church is not cool anymore because there are

too many "weird people" there. Pulling over to help someone with a flat tire is AAA's job, and God forbid we eat at an establishment that doesn't support our political views. We can always find many reasons and excuses for disconnecting and living our private lives. In fact, that's why it's so easy to only see the negative in our world; the more you draw apart from people, the easier it is to spot your differences. Everyone will fall short of your expectations when you have a "me versus them" mentality.

Now I know that in the first few chapters, I mentioned how important it is to avoid being a part of a herd that is not conducive to your growth, but by no means should you live a life of isolation. Again, we'll talk more about the importance of supportive environments later.

The world is made up of many different and imperfect people—broken, hurt, good, evil, wealthy, and poor. I'm willing to bet that you and I aren't as perfect as we like to believe, either. But if we continue to live as if we are, we'll find ourselves misunderstood and alone, craving the very thing we've been running from.

It takes love to see the positive in other people. It takes wisdom to give grace and find common ground. It takes effort to spread light. People are messy and needy. Sometimes, it takes sacrificing your time, lunch, coffee, or money to help someone else in trouble. It takes courage to leave your comfort zone to share your message just so that it might encourage someone else, even when you risk being judged.

And somehow, it seems that we've just about run out of the desire to work with each other, sacrifice for one another, love unconditionally, and have the courage to lead. This is why people are starved for positivity. The world is hungry for people who spread joy, people who sit and cry with the broken-hearted, people who choose to see the best in all things, people who can make us laugh when we haven't laughed in too long, people who show courage when everyone else is paralyzed by fear.

And that's where you and I come in. That's the secret sauce to discovering your life's purpose. If you can find a way to positively "feed" a starving world, you will find your life's purpose. Because when you believe in yourself, you can discover your passions and achieve your dreams, but when you believe in others, you can help them discover and achieve theirs. And this is how you align with your purpose.

Some people will achieve their goals and dreams but might miss the bigger picture and only live to please themselves. Others will dedicate their lives to serving everyone else but will never set their own goals and achieve their dreams. And you can debate which would be better or worse, but I say that true purpose comes when you can do *both*. We are wired for connection, and we can find it in service to one another. Still, at the same time, I believe we are made in the image of someone much greater, and that means that we also have a natural desire to grow, explore, build, invent, use our imagination, and create.

This is why Big Idea #1 is to BELIEVE IN YOURSELF, and Big Idea #2 is to BELIEVE IN OTHERS. They go hand in hand.

If you become everything you could be, and you help others do the same, no matter what it is that you decide to do, you will live with purpose.

Your purpose is to create a positive ripple in the world.

How you do that is entirely up to you. As far as you and I are concerned, a flower serves its purpose because it brings beauty into our world. But as far as the bee is concerned, the same flower serves its purpose because it provides pollen. In the same way, you can serve your family's physical or emotional needs while also making the world a more beautiful place to be just by blooming into the greatest version of yourself.

Don't overthink this; remember that my brothers and I were able to positively impact the world by simply having fun with each other and by finding joy in the little things. Start there. Start with becoming the best person you can be, finding joy in the process, and helping others do the same.

If you're a mother, be the best mom you can possibly be. If you're a school teacher, be the teacher students talk about long into adulthood. If you're a leader, lead with courage, decency, honesty, and humility. Always stay positive, choose to see the best in other people, encourage them, love them, challenge them to pursue their dreams, and pursue yours too. But don't get so caught up in thinking about the future that you forget to live in the present. And by simply being your best self, you will inevitably inspire others to do the same.

There you have it—if you can do even these few things, like the flower, your life will have already served a greater purpose than many lives that have come and gone before you. And if you think I'm oversimplifying this idea of *purpose,* perhaps you're living too much in the mind and not enough in the heart.

When my grandfather, Michael Ivanov, was in the Nazi's Dachau Concentration camp, as you can imagine, there were many days where he felt like giving up. The Nazis worked their prisoners to death. Most days, the prisoners were woken up early in the morning to march out and dig trenches, clean bombed cities, and build new roads. They didn't return to camp until night, only to do it all again the following day. It was hard physical labor that became even more difficult during the winters.

My grandfather said that when he felt like he just couldn't take it another day, he would find ways to serve someone worse off than him. Throughout the day, he would steal an extra sock, handkerchief, or slice of bread and hide it in his jacket. Then, when he returned to camp, he would bring those items to someone bedridden or starving to death. Finding ways to serve someone else gave him a reason to keep living. As long as there was even one person who needed him, there was meaning to his life.

My friend, it doesn't take much to be a positive light and to create positive ripples in the world. There are people who need you. No matter how tough your life may get, someone will always be dealing with something worse. If you can find those people and find a way to lighten their burden, even a little bit, you will experience an immeasurable amount of meaning and self-worth.

Now that you know the foundation of purpose is to love one another, let's dig into your heart a little, find some passions, and identify the dream that is uniquely yours so that you can use your gifts, talents, and abilities to fight for it, achieve it, and have an even greater impact on people.

DEVELOP YOUR PASSIONS

I am sure that many times in your life, in an attempt to

get you to start thinking about your future, teachers, parents, or friends have asked you, "What are you passionate about?" And you likely had no answer. Why?

Because, like purpose, we tend to believe that some lucky people are just gifted with passion. And since maybe you aren't particularly inspired to feed the homeless, save the dolphins, or play the guitar, you think the passion fairy passed you by. So you answer the question, like many people do, "I don't really have any passions."

But the truth is there is no passion fairy. Passions aren't handed out; they are developed. You probably wouldn't be naturally inclined to stop by a nursing home to spend time with old people. (If you are, maybe I'm wrong, and there is a passion fairy.)

But let's say you were invited to an event at a nursing home by a friend who was passionate about serving elderly people, and you reluctantly went. Then, you have a few stimulating conversations with the old people at the event. You realize how valuable their wisdom is to this world. You learn how many wonderful stories and experiences they have to share, and you have a great time. You also see how lonely they are, and you want to help find a solution.

Suddenly, something sparks, and out of nowhere, you have an idea to create a non-profit that helps connect lonely old people to young volunteers who come and spend time with the old people. Suddenly, a little passion is born within you.

Suddenly, you have found a way to serve and love people, and you use your ability to market, connect, network, and build relationships to create a career for yourself—while creating a positive ripple in the world.

You have found your purpose. And it all started with your friend who found and used their purpose to create a positive ripple that helped inspire you! Do you see how that works?

As a kid, I always thought that being *passionate* about something meant I was excited about it. So, I was passionate about swimming, hanging out with friends, and playing football. These were my answers when people asked me about my passions. It wasn't until I started writing my first book and learning to be a professional speaker that I truly understood what passion meant.

The word passion can be described as a strong desire for or devotion to some activity, object, or concept. It won't always be easy, it won't always be fun, it won't always be exciting, but it will always be worth accomplishing because it means something more to you than a simple "fun" activity or goal. There is depth, meaning, and purpose behind a passion.

You know you have a true passion when you can immerse yourself so deeply in an activity that you forget to eat. Or when you can work on something through the night. Or when you can face rejection after rejection, failure after failure, and still show up the next day because you believe in what you are doing. Or when you can lift weights until you cry from pain, but you know the pain is making you stronger.

Passion is what fuels me while writing this book. I have spent countless hours working on this book in coffee shops, my home office, and airports while traveling to different cities. It's not always easy. It takes a lot of concentration and commitment to string words into sentences, sentences into paragraphs, and paragraphs into chapters that make up this book you are holding. Along with the effort it takes to complete this task, there is the fear that comes with putting my thoughts out there for the world to judge and criticize.

Despite all that, it's hard to stop when I sit down to write, and I really get going. Why? Because I am passionate about this project. I enter something psychologists call *the flow state*. This happens when your mind and body are totally absorbed by and intensely focused on something beyond the point of distraction. Your most creative and best self emerges, and magic happens. I am passionate about giving you tools and ideas that will help transform your life like they did mine, and no fear or distraction can stop me from doing that!

Football fans will often say they are passionate about their team. Yes, they scream, shout, dance, or throw beer at the TV, but that's not the kind of passion we are discussing here.

I'm talking about the passion that allows a person with an ordinary upbringing to create and do extraordinary things. The kind of passion that enabled Pablo Picasso to produce his paintings, the kind of passion that helped Og Mandino to write his books and the kind of passion that fuels Elon Musk to build a rocket people can one day fly to Mars.

So, if you have not found that thing, keep searching and never settle!

People make us believe that if we don't decide by the end of our freshman year in high school what we want to do with our lives, we are somehow wasting our lives. Many college students still don't know what they want to do. Many grown adults don't either. Of course, it's never too early to start searching, but it's certainly never too late, either. Some find theirs at ten years old, and some don't see it until they're in their seventies. Colonel Sanders started his Kentucky Fried Chicken franchise in his seventies. The important thing is to keep searching.

It's heartbreaking how many people go through life without ever having something to be passionate about— but spend hours and hours stuck in front of the TV screen. As Viktor Frankl, a psychiatrist and Holocaust survivor, once said, "When a person can't find a deep sense of meaning, they distract themselves with pleasure." Don't distract yourself from that still, small voice calling you out of the darkness and into the light, my friend.

The next time someone invites you to serve, go! The next time someone recommends a good book, read it! The next time you have a quiet moment, sit and think, reflect on your life, and consider why specific experiences, people, or stories stick with you... Inspiration is hidden there.

Often, this is where you will discover a passion for something. As we discussed in Chapter Three about expanding your mind, find ways to also expand your heart, and you will see that you have something more significant to fight for.

COMMIT TO THE PROCESS

A student named Caleb recently approached me after a workshop I held on "finding your purpose." He was a senior in high school and had already completed an extensive law program at his school. He had planned on being a lawyer, or his father wanted him to be one, I don't remember, but now he was questioning if it was what he still wanted to do.

"I'm afraid I just wasted all this time pursuing something that now I don't care much for," he said.

I put my hand on his shoulder. "First, relax," I said. He was tense; I could tell it weighed heavily on him. I reminded him that he had time to decide.

"You are not married to this career path. If you feel like it's not for you, trying something new is okay. It's much worse to commit to doing something that eventually you grow to resent and then hate. At least you explored it."

But what I told Caleb next seemed to make him relax, and I brought a big smile to his face. I told him that some of the most outstanding entrepreneurs in the world have law degrees. So, if he chose to stick with his classes and see this thing through, he would learn an excellent success principle: *commitment to the process.*

I also reminded him that, in the worst case, if he decided later that he would not be a lawyer, the classes he took and the time he spent studying law would be an incredible asset for him in the future, no matter what career he decided to pursue.

Do you think I'm contradicting what I told Caleb about not being married to his career path? Hang with me for a minute.

I reminded him that too many people quit along the way, not because the thing they are pursuing is not the right thing but because it wasn't as easy or quick as they had hoped. So, something that started as a passion became a failure simply because the desire, devotion, and commitment to see it through was not there. Many people still have the definition of passion confused with excitement, like I did when I was young. That's why they quit as soon as they get rejected, fail a few times, and the excitement turns to fear or self-doubt.

Now, you could argue that if someone quits on something, it must not have been a real passion since real passion gives you the strength and ability to persist, according to what we discussed earlier.

The thing is, we evolve, and so do our passions. Remember that discovering your passions is a process, and it's okay for your interests to evolve. Be patient with yourself and embrace the journey of self-discovery. Your desires may change or deepen as you explore new opportunities and gain more life experience. You aren't married to your passions, so you have my permission to evolve.

What doesn't change is your *purpose:* to create positive ripples through love and service to others.

Here's what that can look like: Today, my two biggest passions are writing and speaking, and I fulfill my purpose by using these two passions of mine to create positive ripples in the world. That is my biggest dream being realized. But maybe a few years from now, as I evolve and expand and am entrusted with more talents (more on talents in a later chapter), perhaps my passions will change. And that's okay because now I have the formula down and will continue to apply it throughout my life. In case you missed it, here is the formula:

Passions + Positive Impact through Love and Service = Purpose.

In my first year of college, I took a few semesters of classes studying power utilities. I planned to become a lineman. I would be one of those guys climbing up the telephone pole, fixing the wires after a storm. However, I realized this was not a career I wanted to pursue about half a year into taking those classes and a few field trips to various power plants, substations, and dams. A lineman's peak season is wintertime; they work the most hours when it's cold and wet. I also learned that I would have to be a grunt or a low-level apprentice for years before I could join a union job, which meant living in some remote town in another state in the middle of nowhere before gaining enough experience for a good position.

That was enough for me to change my mind. I knew right away this wasn't a career path for me because I knew I needed to stay close to family, which is much more important to me than any career. The time and sacrifice would be worth it for some people, but I'm not crazy about working in the cold and wet and alone.

So I changed direction, started taking computer classes, and later discovered that most of the power utility credits also transferred to this course. But even if I had wasted those credits, it would still have been worth making that decision because it's better to lose a little time than to pursue something you hate or have no passion for just because you have already started. Never make yourself a prisoner; you don't have to stay stuck.

So many people hate what they do and who they are, but they won't make the hard decision to change course simply because they think it's too late, too scary, or too inconvenient to change. And if that's you, that's okay; that's why I'm here, and we're having this conversation.

It's never too early and never too late to reinvent yourself. That's what life is about: constant change and growth! My only caveat: Make sure you're not jumping to the next thing just because the first thing didn't happen as fast as you wanted.

FIND WHO INSPIRES YOU

Often, your passions will not have anything to do with what you are currently good at. Unless you are in your teens, this won't surprise you. You may have already found this to be true for yourself.

For years, one of the most frustrating things for me was trying to find what I was good at because people would always ask, "Well, what are you good at?" They would tell me that if I knew what I was good at or what my "natural talents" were, I could pursue that.

But how do I know what I am good at when I haven't

tried much of anything? So there I was in my teens, trying to figure out why being good at video games still seemed like a dead end. Like video games, there are tons of fun hobbies out there. But most hobbies won't be true passions. I could also draw very well when I was young, but I wasn't passionate about drawing. It was just something I enjoyed doing to relax. It wasn't something that challenged me to grow or pushed me out of my comfort zone; there was no deeper meaning or drive behind it.

A woman came up after a speaking engagement and asked me how she could excite her son about his natural talents. He was always bored, and she wanted to help him find a passion. She told me that he was good with his trumpet; he was in the school band.

"Maybe he can be a musician," she said. "But he is casual about it. In fact, he's good at many things, but he doesn't seem to care too much about them."

Whether you're trying to nudge your child in the right direction or you're looking for a fresh start in your own life, taking inventory of what you are good at can be a great place to start. Are you more hands-on or mind-oriented? Would you rather spend hours working with tools or typing a story behind a computer? By all means, explore those things.

But I would bet that you will find true passion when you challenge yourself to step into something bigger, something unfamiliar, something that can't be a simple hobby because it requires more of you than you can currently handle. When you engage your mind in something new and unfamiliar, growth happens, and often new passions are discovered. My younger brother and his wife learned how to code on YouTube, and now both work for tech companies based out of Silicon Valley. Something that was interesting but challenging became a passion because the mind was engaged.

I will challenge you like I challenged that lady with her son. Sure, he might play various instruments well, but if those things no longer challenge him, there will be no passion for them. Instead, I told her to ask her son who inspires him and why.

Now let me ask you, who inspires you and why?

We will always be drawn toward people we admire because that is how we orient ourselves in this world. We all have heroes. When we see someone living life in such a way that makes us want to be better, we now have a point of reference. If we are becoming like them, we are headed in the right direction. If we are nothing like them, we can examine ourselves and see what needs to change. This is not about comparing yourself to others but about setting a high standard to strive for.

Show me your heroes and I'll show you your values!

Maybe their songs put words to the anxiety we feel but

can't express. Perhaps their leadership gives us confidence that everything is going to be okay. Maybe their teaching style makes us feel seen, heard, and capable. Maybe their surgery skills saved our life or the life of someone we know. Perhaps their ability to build financial wealth inspires us to do the same for our family. Maybe their speeches and books permitted us to dream again, and we wonder what it would feel like to do that for others. Besides the outward skill or talent of the person, there is usually an underlying deeper reason for why you admire that person; a big clue to discovering your passions is hidden there.

We love watching the James Bond movies; we can all agree they are entertaining. But I believe it goes deeper than entertainment. I think that through the experience of seeing James Bond's daring actions, confident personality, and travels to exotic places worldwide, we secretly hope it's possible for us, too.

If you can pin down exactly why someone inspires you, guess what? It will help you identify what you value. And if you know what is most important to you, you can take a step closer to your purpose.

Think about someone who inspires you.

What quality, ability, or personality do they possess that inspires you? Do they live an adventurous life? Do they make people laugh? Are they a strong leader?

What about them makes you want to be like them? What are they doing that you find yourself wishing you could also do? Are their skills, talents, or passions positively affecting the world? This will give you some significant insights into your desires.

You see, you decide what gives you meaning, and if you are doing things that give your life meaning and creating positive ripples in the world, you are living with purpose!

Writing this book to help you navigate life gives me meaning and joy. This morning, I've been sitting here in my office chair for four hours, hammering away at my keypad, and I haven't been bored for a second. My passion is to inspire others. And because I'm doing things that give my life meaning, and I'm doing something that I am passionate about, I am walking out my purpose.

See how that works? It's much simpler than you have been led to believe. Here is the formula again: Passions + Positive Impact through Love and Service = Purpose.

I know what you're thinking, "Yes, Michael, all of this is true, but I don't have writing talent like you do; I'm not a good speaker, and I'm not good with words."

And that is precisely why you should be moving in that direction! Imagine who you could become if you strived to be more like your heroes. Don't go back to that old thinking pattern that you should only pursue what you are currently "good at" or what comes easy. You don't want easy, trust me. You want adventure. You want a challenge. You want growth. There is no room for growth if you only stick to something you excel at.

I reinvented myself at age twenty-five, seven years after graduating high school, seven years after I was supposed to have had things figured out. I may have to do it again at forty-five and again at fifty-five. This is why I keep stressing that nothing is final in life; you can decide on one thing and change completely a few years later, just as long as you continue to grow and become the best version of yourself. Constantly adapt and reinvent yourself, whether you're still in high school, seven years out, or seventy years out.

One day, after an awful shift at my corporate job, I stopped by the local library on the way home. I wanted some time to sit and think about what the heck I was doing with my life. The library had a little book cart with old, worn books on its shelves that it was trying to get rid of. There, I found that torn and tattered purple copy of, *A Better Way to Live* by Og Mandino—the book I have previously mentioned. I paid one dollar for it—and that was the best investment I have ever made!

The book was what I needed at the time. It gave me hope. It encouraged me to dream big. It reminded me that life was short. It pushed me to think about what exactly I wanted from my life. Og Mandino's journey inspired me so much that then and there, I swore to myself that I was also going to become an author and a motivational speaker. I found the person I admired.

I was not "good" at writing. I had never written anything besides school homework. And I was certainly not a good speaker (remember how I sprinted, terrified, out of my speech class). But I wanted to do what Og Mandino did for others. I wanted to give people perspective and hope, remind them of the brevity of life, and permit them to dream big. When I read that book, I knew what I had to do. When you are ready and open for change, life will put you in the right place at the right time.

A phrase I love goes like this, "We are standing on the shoulders of giants." Extraordinary people throughout history have dealt with and overcome all of the same problems we have and then some. And you and I, generations later, can use their wisdom to gain a deeper understanding of ourselves and achieve more extraordinary things by "standing" on their shoulders. We can use their wisdom, experience, insights, and breakthroughs to see further ahead and achieve even greater things.

If you're stuck, whose shoulders can you climb on? Go back to that person who inspires you. Examine their life: What are or were they doing, how are they living, what kind of legacy did they leave, what is their success advice, how did they get to where they are now, what challenges, obstacles, and fears have they overcome. Then, follow in that person's footsteps.

If you struggle to blaze your trail, start by imitating someone who has gone before you. Read their books and watch their videos. If they are accessible, spend time with them and ask a million questions. And a beautiful thing will happen. At first, all you can do is imitate, but as you grow and move towards your newfound passion, you begin to blaze your own trail by standing on the shoulders of giants.

Og Mandino inspired my writing and speaking styles. I practiced doing speeches just like he did because I needed a structure to work from, someone to imitate. But as I got more comfortable, my personality, experience, and story emerged, and I developed my own voice and style. If I had looked upon his skills and abilities and discounted myself because I was not "good" or "naturally talented" like he, I would not be where I am today. I did not need to be good like he was; I just needed to expand my mind, and my mind took care of the rest.

This is what Big Idea #2 is all about. Remember, there is no predestined purpose for you carved into some stone wall in a cave in the Sahara desert.

If you want to understand why you are here, you need to realize that being alive, being silly in matching flannels, and being a part of your family, school, community, and group of friends is what life is about! Then, what you decide to do for a job, what you choose to do for a career, who you decide to imitate and follow, and what you choose to be passionate about and fight for is entirely up to you.

Your purpose is to be a light in the world. Period. What you choose to do on top of that with your skills, talents, passions, and abilities, is entirely up to you!

It's surprising how little encouragement most people need to keep going and how little they receive. Be that encouragement for people. Be that light and positive ripple in the world. Believe in others.

My friend, now you are ready for Big Idea #3. I'll see you in Chapter Five.

Five

Big Idea #3: THINK BIG

Life can only give you what you ask for, so raise your ambition

A decade or so ago, I woke up at 5:00 AM every morning, put on my tennis shoes, and went for a mile-long walk before the sun was even up. Some days, it was raining so hard that I couldn't see more than ten feet in front of me, and still, I walked the same mile-long loop in a raincoat in the dark. Then, I would change and go to work. I was still working at that printing company back then, and my morning walk was just about the only part of the day I had to myself where I could think clearly.

I did this every day for an entire year. I walked that loop, and I dreamed. I dreamed of having enough money to travel whenever I wanted to. I dreamed of working for myself. I dreamed of quitting my miserable job and helping other people get unstuck. I dreamed of inventing something. I dreamed of creating my very own logo for my very own company. I dreamed of waking up every morning and being excited to jump out of bed. These were all little thoughts that I would entertain in my mind as I walked. I had no idea how to achieve them; I just knew I wanted to change. But I hadn't read Og Mandino's book yet, so my dreams were still all over the place.

But sometimes, wanting change is all you need to start and helps you think, "What else is out there for me?" You can't think and dream big when you hardly take the time to think at all.

You see, if you don't like how things are going in your life right now, you have to get clear on what you don't like and what you will do to change it. Suppose you hate your job, career, where you live, or your inability to pay the bills, but you aren't looking for a solution to these undesirable problems. You are going to remain unhappy, and nothing will change.

The world is full of complainers who have identified everything they hate but have no desire or willpower to do anything about it. Have you ever been around people like that? They're exhausting.

I was clear that I didn't like how my life was going, and I was certainly clear that I wanted to change. But I wasn't yet clear where to go, so I had to keep walking that mile-long loop and fantasize and dream of solutions.

By taking those walks every morning, allowing myself the time to think, and permitting myself to dream, something incredible started to happen. Because I was giving myself time to ponder my life and examine what I didn't like about it, a list started forming in my mind. Even though I wasn't sure exactly where I wanted to go, I could at least get clear on how I would like my life to be different.

My list: I didn't want to be tied to a location, I didn't want to be limited in what I got paid per hour, I didn't want to be limited in the amount of money I could earn in a week, I didn't want to answer to a boss, I didn't want to sit in traffic twice a day, I didn't want to be doing work I did not enjoy, I didn't want people to put deadlines on me, I didn't want to trade hours for dollars, I didn't want to have only two days off a week, I didn't want someone to limit how many vacations I took per year, I didn't want to be limited in how much time I could spend with my wife.

Little by little, as I walked in the rain, snow, fog, and dark, morning after morning, my list grew. And the more my list grew, the bolder it became. The bolder I became. See, if you are going to dream, you might as well dream big. If you are going to ask life for something, you might as well raise the stakes.

I was creating a "What I don't want" list and having fun with it. If no one would see my list anyway, why not think boldly?

Life can't give you something you haven't asked for regarding your dreams. And sometimes, the best way to know what to ask for is first to identify what you don't want.

MAKE A "WHAT I DON'T WANT" LIST

I want to challenge you to create a list of non-negotiables. A list of things you will not settle for, at least not in the long run. Keep your list private—you don't want some small thinker making you feel stupid for asking for what you want.

Of course, there were things I did and still do on my journey as an entrepreneur that I don't want to do, like learning how to edit videos, running advertisements on Facebook, or sending thousands of emails to conference planners. I don't necessarily enjoy doing any of these things, but they are **stepping stones** to what I want, so I do them.

Your "what I don't want" list is by no means a list of things you don't want to do just because you don't feel like it. On the way to your dreams, you will have to do many things you don't exactly "feel" like doing. The purpose of your list is to begin eliminating mediocrity from your life and clarifying what's important to you so that you can find your passions and purpose.

As I have revealed, you have unlimited possibilities, but to discover your passions and purpose, you eventually have to settle on something and put all of yourself into it. As we covered in Chapter Three's Expand, Visualize, and

Believe section, your ideas of what's possible need to change. But if you keep living with "unlimited possibilities," you will always stay in the same place.

My wife knows this all too well. Where we live, there are unlimited possibilities of places to eat. And because we have limitless possibilities, and she knows what she definitely *doesn't* want, she can take far too long to decide what she *does* want.

Eventually, you've got to make a decision and take immediate action!

This list will be as important as your list of goals. Those two lists should go side by side. It was because of my "what I don't want" list that I discovered what I would do with my life after reading Og Mandino's book.

See, I referred to my list whenever I thought of a business or an idea for a different career path. If the potential business idea limited me financially, I would scrap that idea. If the career path would keep me from my family, I would scrap that idea. When I got new job offers, which still required me to sit in traffic twice daily, I would decline them. Because I had my list of non-negotiables, my list of things I would not settle for, out of the hundreds of ideas and opportunities that would come my way, I knew which ones to pursue and which to pass on.

I was beginning to understand the power of thinking big! I was no longer willing to settle to earn a paycheck; I knew there was more for me. And there is more for you, my friend, as long you stop settling for what comes first or what comes easy.

Life will throw you a lot of shiny objects, and people will give you advice and hundreds of ideas on what you should do, but if you have your list of what you don't want in life and your career, you will know which opportunities to pass on.

Then, you can go all in when the right idea comes along and doesn't force you to compromise something on your list.

When the idea of becoming an author and motivational speaker first came to me, I matched it against my list, and I knew I had picked the right dream to pursue.

"Will I be working for myself instead of a boss? Yes!" Check.

"Will I be limited in the amount of income I could earn? No!" Check.

"Will I be able to have my wife and siblings as my business partners? Yes!" Check.

"Will I be able to create my own company and logo and merchandise? Yes!" Check.

"Will I have to sit in traffic twice daily and clock into an office? No!" Check.

"Will I be able to impact other people while doing something fun? Yes!" Check.

"Will this be something I could see myself never wanting to retire from? Yes!" Check.

"Is this something that will continually challenge me and force me to grow? Yes!" Check.

Writing books and speaking around the country did not go against any of the non-negotiables on my list. I was ready to go all in. It's hard to describe how empowering it is when years of confusion and frustration vanish, and your life purpose becomes clear as day.

Thanks to my list of non-negotiables, I suddenly had something to fight for. This will also happen to you, my friend, if you get clear on what you want and don't want.

Start working on your list.

The list will turn your dreams, wishes, hopes, and desires into a concrete declaration. It will be like your very own Declaration of Independence. And when you have a definite statement of what you want and don't want in life, the fears and insecurities lose their grip on you, and your path becomes clear.

As you continue to move towards your dreams and passions, you will gain confidence and develop the courage to slay the "dragons," the fears, insecurities, and doubts that stand in your way. When the desire to achieve a goal becomes strong enough, nothing that stands between you and that desire will be able to stop you. So be bold!

And again, your list is something that will help guide you. It should not stop you from taking a short-term opportunity here and there that might not be the most exciting, fun, or convenient thing at the time, as long as that opportunity is a step in the right direction. You might not enjoy school now, but it is a step in the right direction. You might not like your job at the coffee shop now, but it'll help you save up for a laptop or a car. You might not enjoy sitting in your cubicle, but it can be a stepping stone to your dreams if your vision extends beyond your cubicle walls.

Since I was ten years old, I've worked dozens of odd jobs. I pulled weeds in the hot sun for five bucks an hour. I shoveled manure at a farm for ten hours a day. I delivered newspapers while my friends played video games, I mowed lawns for my neighbors, I slept for two hours a day for an entire semester in college so that I could work at a packaging plant at night and pay for my textbooks, and I framed houses in the pouring rain and scorching sun.

Along the way, you must do what you must to get to where you want to go. People who live aimlessly and suffer in silence without a purpose sacrifice their lives in vain.

Make sure you know where you are going, and none of your sacrifices will be in vain.

Keep working until you can live your life on **your** terms. That's the definition of success... living life on your terms, whatever those terms may be.

BE READY FOR OPPORTUNITIES

Many opportunities in my life came and went, but nothing changed in my life until I was ready for change. See, an opportunity is like a seed. Opportunity does not earn money or happiness or reveal your purpose; it only provides the resources to get those things. Opportunities are resources with potential. What you do with those resources is entirely up to you. You can use them, invest in them, care for them, or squander them. If you want to grow an apple tree, you need a seed. But even if you have a seed, you don't have an apple tree. You have the resource, the potential for an apple tree.

You still have to till the soil and remove rocks, clumps, and roots. Then you have to plant the seed, water it, care for it, and ensure it gets enough sunshine and animals don't dig it out of the ground, and eventually, after all that hard work and patience, you will have an apple tree. Then, you can make apple sauce, apple pies, or whatever else your heart desires. But it all starts with opportunity.

None of us are short of opportunities. If you think you

have no options, you might need a shift in perspective. Opportunity is often disguised. Sometimes, it's disguised as work. Sometimes, it's disguised as an obstacle. Sometimes, it's disguised as a setback. But if you look hard enough and keep a positive mindset, you will see that there are hidden opportunities in every moment, day, and obstacle of life.

I used to believe that growing up poor, being an immigrant, having English as my second language, and being shy and insecure all limited my chances of success. But when I set out to create my dream of writing and speaking, I finally realized how much my humble upbringing and family story was an asset. All of my books, including this one, and all of my speeches include stories from my childhood, stories about my grandfather in the war, stories about my parents trying to make it in America, stories of me running out of my speech class, and stories of me being rejected by girls.

These stories now make my books and speeches relatable and entertaining to audiences as I teach life principles. Stories of setbacks are now my most valuable assets. Every moment and setback in your life is just part of your story. Soon, they will be the very moments you reference as the reason for your success.

When I got the idea to be a speaker and author, I could have said, "No way, what am I going to write and speak about? I have nothing to offer. I'm not famous; who would listen to me or read my books?" And if I'm honest, all those doubts crossed my mind. But because I had been taking those early morning walks, dreaming of success, hoping for something better, reading everything I could get my hands on, and finding inspiring people to learn from, my mind, or my "soil," was prepared for the seed. If I had been complaining about life, wishing it were better but not looking or dreaming of better opportunities, the idea would have just come and gone. I would never have been able to plant the seed in my mind.

You have to be ready. Opportunities are out there, and they are coming. What you do with them is entirely up to you. Cultivate the soil now. Prepare the ground for the seed that is coming. Work on removing those limiting beliefs. Work on your internal dialogue. Work on finding your passions and have something to fight for. And when that seed comes through a book, speaker, or job offer, take it and plant it. It will only take root and thrive in your mind if you have prepared yourself for it.

I know there are thousands of people like me who have had the idea to write books or become motivational speakers but never made it happen. I know this because they reach out to me to ask for my advice on where to begin. But most never take action on my advice, or if they make some effort, they eventually quit. They haven't cultivated the soil because they haven't worked on their mindset. So when they realize how much effort they will have to put in, they become overwhelmed, and suddenly, the big dream doesn't sound so appealing.

That's why you've always got to be working on your mindset. Then, a little hard work and a few fears or limiting beliefs don't deter you from reaching your potential and living purposefully.

My mom read me this parable when I was little. I never forgot it:

> *A farmer went out to sow seeds in his fields. Some fell along the path as he was scattering the seed, and the birds came and ate it up. Some fell on rocky places where they did not have much soil. The plant sprang up quickly because the soil was shallow. But the plants were scorched and withered when the sun came up because they had no roots. Other seeds fell among thorns, which grew up and choked the plants. Still, other seeds fell on good soil, producing a crop—a hundred, sixty, or thirty times what was sown.*

Some people are like the path in the parable. Their mind is so hardened by their life experiences that a new idea can't even take root. "It will never work," they say.

Some people are like the rocky soil. They may be open to new ideas, but they still have too many negative people in their lives, and they let the words of others choke their dreams out.

Some people are like the soil with thorns. They have so many limiting beliefs, fears, habits, and doubts that even if they take action on new ideas or opportunities, the negativity eventually overpowers them.

We all get opportunities. But only those whose mind is like the good soil will have the courage, the mental fortitude, and the willpower to do something with them.

My friend, the fact that you have read this far tells me that your mind will soon be like the good soil. Whatever ideas and opportunities come your way will lead to incredible success, impact, and purpose!

My first big breakthrough into the speaking world came via a local TEDTalks-style event called VANTalks. When I submitted my audition video for the event, I was sure I would be selected as one of the speakers because I had practiced many times before recording. A few weeks later, I got an email. I was not selected. The rejection hurt.

I did not curse the event planners. I did not convince myself that they missed out on me. I did not pretend that I never even wanted to be there in the first place like people often do to save face when rejected.

Instead, when the event day came, I bought a ticket. I sat in the audience, watched the other speakers, and applauded them. I imagined myself on the stage. I visualized myself doing a speech. I even felt the nerves the speakers were feeling. In my mind, I might as well have been up on that stage.

I waited a year, and I submitted another video. But during that year, I did not just wait. I pulled together my own events. I rented a conference room at a local office building and offered my friends free coffee and donuts just to get them to come. I practiced my speech over and over again, and I got better. And I organized more events and was scared each time. That's the power of having a big dream. You are willing to face your fears because the goal becomes more important to you than the fears and insecurities that stand in your way.

I felt more confident when it came time to submit my audition video again. A few weeks later, I got an email inviting me to do a second audition, this time in front of a panel of judges. I had made it to the second round.

I had watched many TED Talks and knew that to stand out and be memorable to the judges; I would have to do something shocking or unexpected. So, when I showed up for my audition, I brought a bag of fifty pairs of shoes with me. While waiting in the lobby for my turn, I chatted with a few others auditioning to speak. One guy laughed at my bag of shoes. He thought I was trying too hard and told me he didn't have a speech prepared; he planned to "talk from the heart" until his time was up.

When my turn came, I stood confidently in front of the judges, delivered my carefully prepared and practiced speech, and dumped the shoes on the floor at the moment where I spoke about teen suicide. The shoes helped me paint a picture of the current year's suicide statistics. Each pair represented a teen who had committed suicide that year.

A week later, I received an email congratulating me on being selected as one of the speakers. Speaking at that event opened the door for me to officially step into the speaking world. The guy who laughed at me was not selected. He did not take the opportunity seriously; he disrespected the process and acted as if he was an obvious choice without putting in the time to prepare. Opportunities are everywhere. It's what you do with them that determines your success or failure.

Are you ready?

Examine your life now. Where have you become hardened to new ideas? Where have you become too proud to be seen starting small? Do you still hang out with people who blame, complain, and gossip? What habits can you change to improve instead of gradually declining in every area of your life? Where are you missing opportunities because of your surroundings or your mindset?

Had I not been expanding my mind by taking those walks, reading books, and dreaming of big things, I may have missed the tiny seed planted into my mind by Og Mandino's book. But because I had been softening my mind to new ideas by removing rocks and clumps and clearing the thorns, the seed landed on good and fertile soil and bore much fruit.

Cultivate your garden. Remember, opportunity often comes in the form of the smallest seed, which might not look like much to the outside world. But when planted in fertile soil, cared for, nurtured, and nourished, it becomes an idea so deeply rooted that nothing can tear it out.

NURTURE YOUR GIFTS, TALENTS, AND ABILITIES.

I'm a big fan of old parables. I wrote an entire book based on another old parable my mom used to teach me called *The Parable of the Talents.*

The great parable does not describe a setting for the story. In my book, *The Servant with One Talent,* I placed the story in ancient Babylon because, in those days, a measure of gold was called a "talent," just like in the parable, and I thought it would be a suitable setting.

The ancient parable goes something like this:

A wealthy businessman once had three servants working for him. One day, he is preparing for a business trip. In those days, to go on a trip, you had to assemble a caravan of camels, carts, supplies, and helpers, especially if you were traveling far and had merchandise to sell. So before he leaves, he calls his three servants together and explains his plan.

He says to them, "I am going on a trip. I will be gone for

a very long time. I have a lot of gold, and I do not want my gold to sit around and collect dust while I am gone." You see, he is brilliant. If invested, he knows that the gold can make even more profit for him. So he turns to the first servant, saying, "I will entrust you with five talents of gold. You are my most loyal servant; you've worked for me the longest, so you get five. Go and invest it, and see what you can accomplish with it. When I return, we will see how you did."

Remember, the servant is being entrusted with a lot of money. One talent of gold in today's money is worth over a million dollars. So he is being tasked with investing roughly five million dollars on the businessman's behalf! It's a good thing to have a lot of responsibility placed on you; it means you have proven you can handle it.

The man turns to the second servant. "For you, I will leave two talents of gold. You haven't worked for me for as long as the first servant, and you're not as experienced, so two should be good enough for you. See what you can do with it. When I return, we will review your numbers and see all you have accomplished."

Then he turns to the third servant. "I will entrust you with one talent of gold. You aren't as experienced; you haven't worked for me as long, but a talent of gold is still plenty. Let's see what you can do with that for now."

The wealthy man leaves and is gone for years. Eventually, he returns. He gathers his servants and invites them to share what they have done with this gold—the money and opportunity he had given them.

He calls up the first servant. "If I remember correctly, I left you with five talents. What have you done with these resources?"

The servant replies, "You gave me five talents. I took that gold, and I invested it in the markets. Eventually, the investment grew, and I received back twice as much as you gave me. The five talents have turned into ten."

The businessman was delighted by this. He invites the second servant and asks him what he has done with the two talents entrusted to him. The servant replies. "You gave me two talents. I invested that gold in the markets just like the other servant. Eventually, the investment grew, and I received back twice as much as you gave me. The two talents have turned into four."

Again, the businessman is pleased. Finally, he invites the third servant and asks what he has done with the one talent entrusted to him. The servant replies, "You gave me one talent. I have never had this sort of money in my life. I did not want to lose it or be robbed and indebted to you. So, at night, I went out behind the city walls into the desert and buried it to keep it safe. And when I found out you were back, I dug it back out, and here it is, right back to you, safe and sound, one talent of gold."

The businessman was furious. The gold could have been

invested and returned with interest. He complains that simply putting the money in the bank could have returned him at least some interest. Instead, the servant did nothing with the opportunity he had been given. The wealthy businessman ordered the talent to be taken from the servant, who was banished from his household.

This story has many lessons and takeaways, but one thing is clear. We all get opportunities. Some of us might get less than others; some of us might get more. But we all have resources available to us. The city you live in, the school you go to, the job you work in, the people you are surrounded by, the air in your lungs, the beat of your heart, and the eyes you are reading with are all gifts you possess. They are like the talents entrusted to you.

And whether it feels like it or not, you have more than some ever will. So don't be so busy comparing to others. If you compare yourself against everyone else, it will always feel like you have less. Don't look at the talents the others have received; look at what you have and use it to the best of your abilities.

One day, my time and your time here on earth will end. When you reflect on your life, will you be happy with how you spent your time? Were you like the servant who received five talents, invested them, and created more? Did you love people and empower them? Did you follow those dreams and achieve them? Did you find your passions, invest in them, live to your greatest potential, and discover your purpose? Or... were you like the servant who received one talent? Did you live in fear and worry, so you took what you had and kept it hidden? Did you bury your passions in the desert, play it "safe," and leave no impact on the people around you?

You see, the servant who received five talents very likely once was given only one. And because he invested it and returned on the investment, he was probably entrusted with two, three, four, and then five the next time. Perhaps he will start with ten in the next opportunity and do even more with it. In life, you and I only get more when we become more. And we can't become more if we keep thinking small or do nothing with what little we have been given. We won't be entrusted with more until we invest in what we already have.

That's what I mean when I challenge you to think big. Think ahead five, ten, fifty years. Won't you regret playing small? Won't you regret not chasing your biggest dreams? Won't your little fears, insecurities, and doubts seem insignificant then? Of course, they will. So don't let them rob you today.

They say the best books have never been written. The best songs have never been sung. The best ideas are buried with the people who took them to the grave with them and never brought them out to the world. They were too afraid of what people would think. They were too scared they might fail. They were too consumed by their insecurities and limiting beliefs. They were too busy pursuing pleasure. They did not cultivate good soil, and the seeds that were scattered around them never flourished. They never invested in their talents.

Maybe all you have known your entire life is poverty. Perhaps you have family in prison or rehab, and you don't feel like you won the lottery in the family department. Maybe the biggest you've ever dreamed is to survive school, get a job, and hopefully be able to pay your bills. And now you realize you should have dreamed bigger. Perhaps you're consumed in worry about your debt. Maybe all you can focus on is making it through another day without ending it all.

But right now, for this moment, I am challenging you to think big, to lift your eyes beyond these current limitations and look at what's possible. You are capable of so much more.

You don't have to start with five talents to do big things. Start with one. Start with what you have now, and it is only a matter of time until you will be entrusted with opportunities you have only once dreamed of. You don't need to have everything figured out to get to where you want to go; you have to start.

My friend, now you are ready for Big Idea #4. I'll see you in Chapter Six.

Six

Big Idea #4: NEVER EVER GIVE UP

Life is going to test you; how bad do you want it?

When I was seventeen, my older brothers and I were going to a friend's wedding. Andrey was driving his Mitsubishi Montero, Igor was in the passenger seat, and I was in the back seat. Somewhere along the way, we got into a bit of a road rage with a lady in a pickup truck. She had not seen us and tried to merge into our lane; when my brother Andrey sped up to escape her blind spot, she swerved back into her lane. Apparently, this was too much aggression for her because she caught up to us later down the freeway, threw a lug nut at our car, and proceeded to try and cut us off.

Andrey had had enough of her antics and decided to lose her in traffic. He stepped on the gas pedal and merged into the fast lane on the freeway. We were driving about eighty miles per hour down the fast lane when the crazy lady caught up to us, swerved across three lanes of traffic, and rammed her pickup truck into the back of our car.

Since we were still moving at eighty miles per hour, the entire SUV spun around, the back left tire snapped off, and we started rolling down the freeway. I was unbuckled in the back seat. I remember being in the air as the car rolled and the sound of metal on concrete screeched through my ears repeatedly. I swear it happened in slow motion. I tried to grab onto seats, anything I could get my hands on, to keep from flying out of the car.

Whenever I think back on those few terrifying seconds, I always remember one particular memory. I am in the air, and I am looking down. The car seats are above me, the roof is below me, and I can see the concrete road passing through a shattered window. And I remember the thought I had at that moment: "Wow, this is it. I can't believe this is it. I will be dead any moment now." The feeling can only be described in one word: sickening.

Finally, the car landed on its roof, and we skidded for roughly fifty yards upside down before slamming into a guardrail, eventually coming to a stop. I can still hear the sound of liquids pouring from the engine, my two brothers shouting my name, asking if I am okay. And then scrambling to crawl out of the car because I was sure it was on fire.

When we all crawled out of the car, we were covered in broken glass and our clothes were torn, but we were all okay. It was a miracle. When the ambulance lady came running to us, she looked at the car, then at us, and then said, "Y'all are golden boys! Nobody should have made it out of that car alive."

The roof was caved into the door panels, and the Mitsubishi Montero was so mangled it looked like it had gone through one of those crushing machines at a junkyard.

That was the first time I had ever thought about dying, and I was not too fond of the feeling it gave me. At seventeen years old, I suddenly understood that I was not invincible. Death was not for old people only. I could have been gone if I had been thrown out of the window a few inches to the left, or the car's weight could have squashed me if I landed a few inches to the right.

I thought about my life deeply that week. In psychology, there is something called "Mortality Motivation." This comes when you have a near-death experience. It might be after an accident, receiving some bad news about your health, or losing someone close to you. It makes you realize that we all have a finite amount of time and never know when our time is up. It gives us clarity. It makes us think about how we have spent our time, how we have been treating people, where we've been wasting our time and energy, and ideas on how we could live differently from now on.

And I had that... for about seven days. But a week later, all the emotions had faded, and the accident had mostly left my mind. Nothing changed about the way I was living or treating people.

Motivation is a good thing. Motivation is like a spark that

can light a massive, unquenchable fire. But motivation is not a long-term answer because it comes and goes. I nearly died, and the motivation didn't even last a week. It is just a feeling, and feelings fade. I tell people all the time when I speak on this principle. I tell people that motivation is just the spark, and it needs to lead to an action, a commitment, and the action can lead to breakthroughs. And that's why you can't rely on motivation.

Motivation can start something, but it takes action, persistence, and new beliefs and habits to bring about real change. Trust me, there will be many times when you don't "feel" motivated. I procrastinated working on this book. I knew I needed to get it done, and I believed in the ideas I wanted to write about, but peeling myself away from distractions, silencing the doubts, and sitting down to write wasn't always fun. The whole process was a bit daunting at times. In those moments, I certainly did not "feel" motivated.

On the way to your dreams, there will be days you will not want to even crawl out of bed. Sure, you might have a dream, but the upcoming tasks might become overwhelming, and you would rather stay in bed than face them. But taking action on your ideas is the only way to see results in your life. So, if you can throw your legs out of bed, you will already be making some progress.

TAKE ACTION

William Shakespeare once said, "Our doubts are traitors, and make us lose the good we oft might win, by fearing to attempt."

Taking action is not hard. It's as easy as putting on your pants and stepping out of your house. It really is. Most people overthink everything. Myself included. I have learned that I need to act quickly and consistently to succeed. And even if my steps aren't always wise, I realized I can constantly adjust as I move. If I take immediate action on new ideas, no matter how scared, confused, or unsure I am, breakthroughs happen. There is magic around a person on the move.

Too many people suffer from **paralysis by analysis.** They sit and overanalyze everything. They imagine the worst-case scenario, they create imaginary obstacles in their minds, or they need to see every step of the way to their dreams unfold in front of them before they take a step in any direction. They need to know *precisely* how it will all play out. They are looking for *certainty.*

But guess what? You will never have certainty because pursuing a dream is much more like walking through a maze and a lot less like taking a flight of steps. Half the time, you'll have no idea where to go next. The next opportunity will not always be clear. It will not be orderly and obvious, like walking up a staircase.

In fact, the next step is often around a corner, down a long hallway, or in a hidden door. Often, it will lead you to a dead end, and sometimes, you'll have to go back and restart. That's why you have to keep moving. That's why you have to take the first step, the second one, and the third one, and then you might be able to see around the corner for one more and the next one after that. This is why so many people plop down in one place, paralyzed! They just aren't willing to walk by faith.

Give me any business idea, dream, or career path you would like to pursue, and within minutes, I can give you a short list of actions to take toward that thing. Not because I'm a genius but because I know everything has a process. I don't have to know everything about every path to at least find the first step.

For instance, people often ask me how to write a book. My first question is, "Have you opened a Word document and typed a title or a chapter name? Or jotted down some main ideas you would like to cover in the book?"

Most often, the answer is "No. But it's all in my head."

They also tend to say things like: "I haven't started because I want to know if I should get the book idea copyrighted first." "How should I publish it?" "How do you market a book?" "How do you find a literary agent?" "Should I have my editor sign a Non-Disclosure Agreement?"

They haven't put a single word down on paper and are already worrying about things that are completely irrelevant at this point. These are good things to think about, but not before you've taken the first step. This is why they never write the book—the process overwhelms them. It's too much to handle, and they bury that idea in their "desert."

Of course, all that stuff is too much to handle at first; I had a heck of a time figuring it all out myself when I was starting. But I focused on one step at a time, and another, and the next.

How do you eat an elephant? One bite at a time!

Too many people suffer from paralysis by analysis.

My wife recently got very passionate about homesteading. She grows vegetables, cooks with them, cans them, pickles them, and even makes medicines with them. It's truly a passion for her. She reads tons of books, watches hours of YouTube videos, and studies all the little details of growing a garden, making medicine, and living off the land.

Recently, though, she took it to the next level and started talking about buying a cow to have her raw milk instead of buying milk at the store. I laughed until I realized she was dead serious. Of course, we cannot buy a cow now. We would need a barn and a pasture for the cow to roam and graze, and it would likely turn into a full-time job for me. I am not interested in becoming a farmer at the moment.

But my wife has learned about taking action on her ideas. Even though we aren't ready to buy a cow, she figured out a way to make her dream happen, at least temporarily. She bought something called a "cow share." It's when you pool some money together with people and pay for a cow that you all take turns milking. So now, she goes to a farm and milks "Crema," the cow she partially owns, every Wednesday. I didn't even know there was such a thing as owning a "part" of a cow.

You see, my friend, the mindset is what matters most. If you want something badly enough and are willing to act, you can make it happen. Someday we will get my wife a cow, but for now, she gets gallons of raw milk every week, and we don't have to build a barn or shovel poop. Start with where you are, start with what you have, and start now! Take action.

ALWAYS PERSIST

It requires no particular skill, luck, or talent to be consistent and persistent. If you can be consistent and persistent, you can be anything. Persistence creates momentum, and momentum is an incredible thing. I played "safety" on a local semi-pro football team for several years. It's a challenging position because, often, you are the last line of defense between the ball carrier and the end zone. And if you have a muscular running back with thighs like a bull charging at you at full speed while you are flat-footed on the turf, and the only thing standing between him and a touchdown is you, guess what? You are getting knocked on your butt. If he has momentum, it will be nearly impossible for you to stop him.

But just like physical momentum, you can also gain mental and emotional momentum through persistence. If you consistently take little steps toward your goals, you will grow in confidence, hone your skills and abilities, and become better and more equipped as time passes and obstacles are overcome. Eventually, you, too, will become like that running back; nothing that stands in between you and your dreams can stop you.

Someone once said that the definition of insanity is doing the same thing repeatedly and expecting a different result. Many believe persistence is like ramming your head against a brick wall until it eventually breaks down. They think you must keep doing the same thing until you get the desired result. My friend, that is not what it means to be persistent.

Persistence means trying something, and if you do not get

the desired result, you come up with a new or different strategy and come back and try again. It's about *committing* to the dream, regardless of how many times you are rejected, how many times you fail, how many times you have to reinvent yourself, or how many times you have to come back.

The most important thing is to keep growing in the process. If you fail an exam, it's not a good idea to retake it immediately. Wouldn't it be better to go and study a bit more before you try again? To look up the questions you struggled with and refresh your mind? Of course, it would be.

That's all I'm asking for here. I'm asking you for a commitment to your dream; part of that commitment requires you to improve yourself continually. With every failure, you can learn something new. With every rejection, you can pick up another piece of information. Then, you work on those few things and return to try again.

Remember, rejection is an opportunity for a course correction. When I was rejected for that speaking event I so badly wanted to be a part of, I could have quit and told myself that either it would never happen for me or acted like a victim and made up some story for why I wasn't selected. Instead, I got better. I didn't look at the rejection as an attempt by the event planners to hurt me; I looked at the rejection as a sign that there were things I could improve on.

I had committed to the dream. I had no choice other than to keep getting better and trying. If I had let my pride get in the way back then, I might have forfeited all my dreams.

Eventually, I became more confident speaking to people. I put together my own events and practiced, worked on my stories, learned how to structure a speech, and started to get great feedback. I was beginning to gain momentum. My confidence grew. I learned to trust myself. And my hands weren't shaking so much while speaking. I learned to trust the process. Then, like that running back, I set my sights on the end zone, and there were no fears, past failures, or negative comments from other people that could stop me anymore. The momentum I had gained carried me over all the obstacles between me and where I wanted to go.

See, it's important to remember that obstacles will always be there. Fears will always be there. The naysayers will always be there. But if you have been taking action and persisting, your momentum will push you through everything that tries to keep you from your dreams.

That is persistence.

Rejection is an opportunity for a course correction.

DEVELOP POSITIVE HABITS

With eight boys growing up in the household, my dad learned quickly that if he could keep us busy, we would be more likely to stay out of trouble. So he put us to work! Saturday mornings were the only days we could sleep in because we got up early for church on Sundays and had school Monday through Friday. But one Saturday morning, my dad woke us boys early to help him cut down trees in our backyard.

He was cutting trees with his chainsaw, and our job was to follow behind him, clean up, and stack the wood. We were griping, complaining, and dragging our feet; we wanted to sleep in on the only day we had off. Finally, he got tired of our constant complaining and set his chainsaw down. He gathered us around and looked at each of us for a few seconds before saying, "You are my boys, and it doesn't matter to me how much you gripe and complain and how lazy you are. At the end of the day, I'm your dad, I will still love you the same. But," he went on, "one day you will have jobs, and you will have a boss, or maybe you will be the boss, and you will have employees. Then, it will not be okay to gripe, complain, and be lazy. In the real world, people will not have the same grace for your complaining as I do now. Never let your boss catch you with your hands in your pockets, standing around. Or if you are the boss, never let your employees catch you with your feet up on the table."

Then he told us something I've remembered to this day. He said, "If you're at work and have nothing to do, don't stand around. Pick up a broom and sweep!"

Pick up a broom and sweep. It's such a simple lesson. My dad was not trying to teach us to become the best sweepers in the world; that wasn't the point. He was teaching us a lesson about work ethic, attitude, mindset, and leadership. He taught us at a young age that it's not okay to stand around with your hands in your pockets while others are working. He was showing us that there is always something you could be doing to improve your life, even if it's the most minor and seemingly insignificant thing. You won't get big opportunities if you're chilling with your hands in your pockets. Opportunities come to those who are busy working and trying and expanding.

You can't get the best out of your people if you are a leader who likes to kick your feet up on the desk and make others work. Leaders inspire by setting the tone and leading the pack purposefully, not cracking a whip from the back.

If you avoid work and responsibilities, take shortcuts, and take the easy path, it will bleed into every aspect of your life. But, if you adopt the "pick up a broom and sweep" mentality, you will develop incredible habits that will put you on the track to success.

I can tell you without a doubt that the lesson my dad

taught that day still affects how I approach my life. When I don't know what to do next, I "pick up a broom and sweep." I take care of what is in front of me first, and the next step usually presents itself.

If you've gotten into financial trouble, the same way you got yourself into that mess is the same way you can get out—one choice, one step, and one sweep at a time. If you've messed up your relationships, lost control of your weight, stopped taking care of your body, filled your head with negative news and content, or became lazy with your school work or at your job, these habits will continue to chip away at your potential success and ultimately rob you of a purpose-filled life. I call them the *cavities of life.*

The cavities of life are those little problems you neglect to care for for one reason or another that eventually become big problems you can no longer avoid. Just like a cavity in your tooth will eventually rot to the point it compromises the entire tooth, the little things that initially seem meaningless and insignificant will eventually cause much more pain for you.

So, my challenge for you is to *pick up a broom and sweep!*

Start with the most minor thing you can fix or change. Then, add another and another to the list, and before you know it, you will have developed habits that are moving you toward the greatest version of yourself. Tiny, seemingly insignificant choices and decisions compounded over time become habits and shape your life. And the best part is, when people around you see you busy sweeping up your life, they become inspired to do the same.

Pick up a broom and sweep.

NEVER BLAME OR COMPLAIN

Whether you grew up in a Christian family like I did or have never set foot into a church, you likely have heard the story of Moses leading the Israelites through the desert.

Here's a refresher: At the time, the Egyptian leader, Pharaoh, had made slaves of the Jewish people and was badly mistreating them. Moses, who was himself a Jew but was adopted into the royal family as a baby, eventually left the palace and became a leader of the Jews. Time and time again, Moses petitioned Pharaoh to release the Jews from captivity so that the entire nation of Israelites could leave Egypt and live in the "promised land."

After enduring many visits by Moses and plagues sent by God that decimated Egypt, Pharaoh reluctantly agreed to release the Jews, and their journey through the desert began. Within forty days, they reached the promised land, but because the Canaanites were living there, the Israelites began to doubt that they could ever enter. They started complaining to Moses and blaming him for leading them out of Egypt. They said that it would have been better for them to die as slaves in Egypt than to die free in the desert. They shook their fists at Moses and God, who had promised the land for their nation.

As the story goes, all this blaming and complaining by the entire nation angered God. He told Moses to turn the nation around and send them back into the desert until the whole generation of complainers died. They would not set foot into the promised land.

The moral of the story: Complaining is contagious! If you spend too much time around complainers, they'll keep you from the promised land.

This story is one of my favorites. I have noticed that many times in my life—despite my desire to achieve my dreams, live with purpose, and do great things—I have resorted to blaming and complaining when things didn't go my way. I wonder how often I was at the doorsteps of the promised land, only to be sent back out into the desert because of my attitude.

It's easy to be giving, helpful, enthusiastic, and cheerful when life is going swimmingly, but who are you when things get bad? Who are you when things fall apart? Do you point fingers at the people you perceive to be your enemies? Do you point fingers at your family who doesn't support you in the way you would like? Do you ask, "Why me?" Do you spend time with people who complain and blame? Because if you do, eventually, they'll rub off on you.

Your true character is determined by how you respond to adversity and not by how you handle success. On the way to your dreams, there will be much trouble. How will you respond? Will you spit in the face of those trying to lead you to the promised land? Will you complain and blame and look back on your life and wish you were back at your old job—purposeless, enslaved, but at least safe?

When adversity strikes, Jim Rohn has the best advice: "Don't wish it were easier; wish you were better." Don't wish for an easier life; hope for the strength to overcome and become better equipped to handle your adversity; your dreams are waiting in the promised land.

Your true character is determined by how you respond to adversity and not by how you handle success.

BUILD YOUR CASTLE

Do you remember that game show, "Wipeout?" The contestants try to complete the obstacle course by jumping on the big bouncy balls, dodging swinging arms, crawling over the inflatable soapy staircase, and scrambling through the mud pit, among tons of other obstacles, all while trying not to get knocked out by the hidden giant fist along the way.

Well, that obstacle course is a pretty good representation of life. On the way to your dreams, life will knock you down. It will disorient you with cold water, stumble you with hidden potholes, cause you to slip on soapy staircases, and just when you think you're going to reach the top of the inflatable mountain, a giant padded fist will sock you in the face and send you all the way back down.

You and I have faced (and will face) our share of obstacles along the way. That's inevitable. We'll fall out of our bunk beds, kids at school will make fun of us, bullies will steal our bikes, we'll break an arm or a leg, we'll fail a class, a crush will reject us, a teacher will make us feel stupid, our car will break down and leave us on the side of the road, our parents might get divorced, a friend might become an enemy, a dream might get shattered, a business partner might steal our money, we might find and then lose our love, the economy might tank, our house might get repossessed, we might lose a family member, our health may deteriorate, and on and on until the day we die. From minor inconveniences to life-altering punches, we *all* face obstacles.

Besides learning to develop a strong character through adversity, it's also essential to have somebody we can lean on when we can't possibly walk alone. The most dangerous thing you can do is attempt to take on life's punches alone. You were never meant to.

Yes, I know you are strong. Yes, I know you are resilient. Yes, I know you have a lot to prove. Yes, I know you have a strong sense of pride.

But like that song we all shout at the top of our lungs when it comes on, eventually, "We all need somebody to lean on!"

World leaders have rooms full of advisors. The best athletes in the world have teammates and mentors. Successful entrepreneurs have masterminds and life coaches. Successful marriages have two people who are supportive, honest, and full of love for one another. Strong friendships have people who are there for each other in the good and, most importantly, the bad times.

You need people you love and trust in your life to help you navigate life, to help you handle the losses of life, and to remind you to celebrate the wins. Isolation is a cold, lonely road to misery. Without somebody to lean on, life can crush you.

Remember, we are herd animals. You and I are wired for human connection. Just like your body needs air, food, and water to live, your spirit needs love and connection to thrive. Without it, it withers and dies. Life is flavorless and colorless when we are alone.

In the thirteenth century, German King Frederick II wanted to know what language children would naturally grow up to speak if they never heard anyone speaking around them as babies. He conducted a terrible experiment to find out.

King Frederick placed newborn babies from orphanages in the care of nurses who were forbidden to speak within earshot of the infants. In fact, the nurses were even forbidden to touch the infants. So, what language did they end up speaking? The babies grew up to speak no language because they all died.

This idiotic experiment didn't prove anything about language but proved something else about human nature: The power of touch, love, and connection.

When we have someone to hug, love, share moments with, have conversations with, laugh, cry, and navigate life together, we heal our spirit and, in turn, our bodies. But when we become isolated, it's easier to become resentful, hostile, angry, depressed, and cynical; we develop diseases, suffer, and die before our time.

Imagine the widow who is suddenly forced to take on the world without her husband but has no other support or community around her. How can she have the courage to climb out of bed in the morning amid a tragedy if she has no one to shoulder that weight with her? I would say it is nearly impossible.

And how much less enjoyable are life's wins when no one cheers for us?

My wife is the first person I look for when I step off the stage after a big speech. I swear she is more excited for me than I am for myself. We celebrate that win together. When I publish a book, MaKenzie is the first to read it, and we celebrate that win together. And when there are moments in my life where I do not know what to do and begin to doubt myself, guess who is right there by my side, reminding me of my abilities? MaKenzie. When I get rejected or fail big, guess who is there by my side reminding me to keep going? MaKenzie.

I've told you about my relationship with my brothers. My favorite hangouts are the simple evenings when my brothers and a few close friends come over for an evening around the fire pit. I'll take those over a fancy party any day. An evening spent staring at the fire, laughing, dreaming, and reflecting does more for the spirit than any medicine or therapy ever can. That is my happy place.

In medieval times, people built castles to protect their cities from danger. In peaceful times, the citizens did not stay within the castle walls. They traveled, farmed, and carried on with their lives without special attention to the castle. But the castle was always there, prepared for the days when trouble came. And when trouble did arise, everyone ran through the castle gates for protection. The gates were closed, and the people were safe.

It is best to build your castle when times are peaceful and good. You need something and someone to run to when trouble comes. Create a positive environment to chill and reset in. Surround yourself with people who will stand with you when trouble comes. Establish routines you turn to in order to get you back on track in your life. Develop "fortified" places you can run to find peace, comfort, and protection from the world that is seemingly always trying to undermine your greatness. If you don't, the time to build is now!

And don't forget the heaviest burdens you will ever carry are the thoughts in your head. Please do not try to carry them alone. I bring everything to my "castle." My castle is my wife, family, friends, and faith in God. I run to it when I sense danger or uncertainty on the horizon. I run to it when I am filled with joy and victory and want someone to celebrate with me.

***

The ambulance driver who proclaimed my brothers and me "Golden Boys" had it right. But we aren't "Golden Boys" because there is some particular reason for our lives to be spared more than anyone else's. You, too, are Golden! There is a unique purpose for your life.

My friend, sometimes they will punch you in the face.

This does not mean something is wrong with you; they just want you to quit. So don't ever give up, and just keep going.

When they say you're not smart enough or you don't have what it takes, don't take the bait! Don't settle for mediocrity—this is an opportunity for you to fight harder than ever before, so just keep growing.

When that boy or that girl tells you you're too short for them, have a good cry. But then wipe the tears and find someone a few inches shorter than you, so just keep searching!

If you black out during a speech and run away in fear and humiliation, gather your courage, come back, and try again. And you never know—you just might be invited to a stage you never dreamed of being on. So, just keep coming back.

The world needs you. The world needs your gifts, skills, talents, and abilities. The world needs the gold you have buried deep inside of you. Don't rob us all of the gift only you can bring.

1. Believe in yourself.

2. Believe in others.

3. Think big.

4. And never ever give up!

This is why I'm here, and this is why you are here.

About the Author

Michael is a Game-Changing speaker and Best-Selling author who has impacted thousands of people with his message of resilience.

From students, to athletes, to leaders, to business professionals, Michael motivates audiences to take personal responsibility for their lives, reconnect to their purpose, and cultivate success in every aspect of their lives. As a child, he immigrated to the United States just before the collapse of the Soviet Union and the end of the Cold War and is the grandson of a 'Siege of

Leningrad' and Dachau camp survivor. Michael's talent for story-telling and his success principles motivate and empower audiences to smash fears, limitations, and passive, excuse-oriented mindsets. He reveals how the personal choices we make, the attitudes we carry, and the principles we choose to live by, determine the success & quality of our lives.

If you would like to have Michael speak at your event, please visit Michael's website here:

WWW.SPEAKLIFE365.COM

Be sure to find Michael's other books:

The Mount of Olives:
11 Declarations to an Extraordinary Life

Combining courage, faith, wisdom and wonder into an inspiring tale of self-discovery, The Mount of Olives takes readers for an emotional ride through the life of a boy whose search for better becomes a discovery of something extraordinary. Michael Ivanov's masterpiece tells the story of Felix, the Roman boy who despite all opposition, yearns to gain a worldly treasure. His journey will lead him to riches far different—and far more satisfying—than he ever imagined. Felix's quest teaches us the essential wisdom of listening to our hearts, recognizing opportunity and learning the golden principles strewn along life's path, and, most importantly, to follow our dreams.

The Traveler's Secret:
Ancient Proverbs for Better Living

The Traveler's Secret offers an ancient story of one man's choices—and the principles that make the difference between failure and success. In this fable about following dreams, Michael V. Ivanov's latest masterpiece reveals the journey of Agisillus, a vagabond in ancient Gaul, and his extraordinary encounter with a mysterious traveler. This book reveals secrets to living an extraordinary and purposeful life, amassing personal wealth, and leaving a legacy that continues to sow seeds of life into the world. It shares the ancient proverbs of the wise and the foolish and teaches the universal laws of prosperity. Author Michael V. Ivanov provides concrete advice for living a wise and purposeful life.

The four scrolls:

Scroll 1 The Cultivation

Scroll 2 The Burial

Scroll 3 The Resurrection

Scroll 4 The Harvest.

The Servant With One Talent: Five Success Principles from the Greatest Parable Ever Told

To bring your dreams and desires to fulfillment, you must invest in your talents. This book shows you how to become successful and live with purpose by sharing the secrets hidden in an ancient parable, which holds the universal laws of prosperity.

The Servant With One Talent is an instant classic that holds the key to all you desire and everything you wish to accomplish. Through the story of the unprofitable and lazy servant in ancient Babylon, Michael V. Ivanov provides a unique perspective on the classic parable of the talents. This book provides concrete advice for creating a successful and purposeful life while fulfilling your destiny and becoming the person you were created to be. While many people are burying their dreams, talents, skills and abilities in the desert, like the unprofitable servant did at the beginning of this story, the successful are investing into their skills, talents, and abilities.

The Five success principles in The Servant With One Talent:
1. To each, according to his abilities.
2. A talent buried is a talent lost.
3. Do not concern yourself with your neighbor's wages
4. The time is now.
5. To those who have, much more will be given, from those who have not, what little they have will be taken from them.

The Cabin at the End of the Train:
A Story About Pursuing Dreams

From a chance meeting with a remarkable old man by the name of "Carl," a mysterious WWII veteran who shows up on the train at just the right time, The Cabin at the End of the Train provides 12 priceless lessons about purpose, life, and the importance of perspectives.

The Cabin at the end of the train will provide you with:
-A better understanding of life's challenges and proper perspective for tackling them.
-Practical yet powerful methods of motivation, encouragement, and resolve for those struggling.

-A fresh and insightful perspective on how people can change their view of the world, find strength, and move beyond their problems.

Get signed copies of all of Michael's books at
WWW.MOUNTOFOLIVESBOOK.COM

Made in the USA
Columbia, SC
28 November 2023